A COLORED MAN ROUND THE WORLD

DAVID F. DORR

A Colored Man
Round the World

Edited by Malini Johar Schueller

Ann Arbor

THE UNIVERSITY OF MICHIGAN PRESS

For John, Divik, Maya, and Neena
and Usha Johar

Copyright © by the University of Michigan 1999
All rights reserved
Published in the United States of America by
The University of Michigan Press
Manufactured in the United States of America
♾ Printed on acid-free paper

2002   2001   2000   1999   4   3   2   1

*A CIP catalog record for this book is available
from the British Library.*

Library of Congress Cataloging-in-Publication Data

Dorr, David F.
   A colored man round the world / David F. Dorr : edited by Malini
Johar Schueller.
      p.   cm.
   Originally published: Cleveland, Ohio : Printed for the Author,
1858. With a new introduction.
   Includes bibliographical references.
   ISBN 0-472-09694-X (cloth : alk. paper). — ISBN 0-472-06694-3
(pbk. : alk. paper)
   1. Europe Descriptioin and travel.   2. Middle East Description and
travel.   3. Dorr, David F.—Journeys—Europe.   4. Dorr, David F.—
Journeys—Middle East.   5. Afro-Americans Biography.
I. Schueller, Malini Johar, 1957– .   II. Title.
D975.D72   1999
914.04′28—dc21   99-31471
                                                            CIP

ACKNOWLEDGMENTS

I have drawn upon the help of many people in preparing this manuscript. If it had not been for the immediate encouragement of LeAnn Fields, executive editor at the University of Michigan Press, I would not have started this project. The students in my fall 1997 graduate seminar, "Nineteenth-Century Racial Formations," Mark Adams, Henry Butler, Bradley Dilger, Youlanda Freeman, James Gentry, and Kim Martin, all read *A Colored Man Round the World* and offered good advice on what was needed in the introduction and annotations. I particularly want to thank Bradley Dilger for doing a thorough reading of the text.

Bertram Wyatt-Brown has been a wonderful colleague. He gave me invaluable suggestions for researching Dorr's life and responded promptly to my numerous e-mail queries. John Grabowski and Ann Sindelar of the Western Reserve Historical Society were extremely helpful in enabling me to find materials on Dorr during my visit to Cleveland. Ellen Harrington did the necessary research on Fellowes and Dorr at the Wilson Research Center at New Orleans. John Leavey checked all the French annotations and helped me with many of the complicated ones. Carol Murphy kindly sorted out the Creole French for me. Tom Gallant provided assistance with some of the historical annotations. I also wish to thank Carla Peterson for giving me sound research advice.

CONTENTS

INTRODUCTION
Malini Johar Schueller

Can a slave write a travel narrative? To even pose the question is to bring together fundamentally unequal rights of access: those available to a slave and those available to a citizen free to travel. The *Dred Scott v. Sanford* decision of 1856 had made these inequalities abundantly clear. Even free blacks whose remote ancestors had been brought to the country as slaves were not, and were never intended to be, included as "citizens" of the United States. The movement of slaves from the South to the free states was therefore simply the movement of a slaveowner's property, a right protected by the Constitution.[1] Travel, however, implies a certain freedom of mobility and access to sights and cultural spaces that then get reported in travel narratives. This does not mean that slaves did not travel but rather that their travel was circumscribed by the fact that they were part of an entourage; they waited on their masters or looked after his children. Slaves, like the servants of Victorian bourgeois travelers, scarcely ever achieved the status of "travelers," the power to comment and interpret being largely an "Anglo" privilege, one involved in the production of what Mary Louise Pratt has called Eurocentered forms of planetary consciousness.[2] Being a traveler meant assuming mobility and the complex network of race, class, and gender privileges accruing a genteel (Anglo) identity. It is not surprising, therefore, that most antebellum African-American travel narratives are accounts of travel by escaped slaves, freeborn African-Americans, and newly freed slaves, all of whom had mobility, albeit of a highly contingent sort, and who could, through the displacement of travel, aspire to certain forms of privilege.

But even when they did have the freedom to travel (a free-dom experienced emotionally only outside the boundaries of the United States) and to appropriate different forms of identity, African-Americans wrote travel narratives that were substantially different from those of their white counterparts. Anglo-American travel writers appealed to the curiosity and genteel Europhilia of their readers when writing about Europe, and their desires for exoticism or Christian pity when writing about the Orient or Africa. Some wrote as proud Americans, reverent of Old World history, but contemptuous of the European present, a tendency satirized by Mark Twain in his 1869 travelogue, *The Innocents Abroad.* African-American travel writers, on the other hand, even if they were occasionally Europhilic like William Wells Brown or Nancy Prince, used their changed vantage points as sites from which to rearticulate and refashion arguments against the dehu-manizing effects of slavery and the degrading treatment of Afri-can-Americans in the home country, particularly in comparison with the relative humanity afforded black peoples overseas. African-American travel writing, in other words, substantially foregrounded its exhortatory purpose, whereas Anglo-American travel writing largely presented itself as a vehicle of entertain-ment and cultural consumption, and projected the travel writer as privileged gentleman.

David F. Dorr's *A Colored Man Round the World* (1858) is a unique cultural and literary text because it challenges the racial aesthetics and ideologies that separate Anglo and African-Ameri-can writing in the antebellum period. By subverting the hege-monic black-white racial definitions of the dominant culture, Dorr asserts the right of African-Americans to fashion varied identi-ties and also questions the class assumptions of antebellum white identity.[3] *A Colored Man Round the World* points to the hetero-geneity of antebellum African-American writing, the importance of regionalism in a consideration of this writing, and the variety of forms of African-American protest writing. It also questions the idea of slavery as a uniform experience.

Like many Anglo-American writers, Dorr uses travel writing to project a leisurely, gentlemanly self and to fashion an aristocratic selfhood through the display of inherited "cultural capital."[4] Thus Dorr presents to his readers a panorama of the history, culture, and customs of the countries he visits, pausing to convey his enchantment with particular artifacts. Although he makes his slave status clear early in the text, Dorr critiques slavery and slaveowners through the lens of taste, the symbolic expression of class position, rather than simply through moral parameters.[5] Like many radical African-American thinkers such as David Walker and Henry Highland Garnet, Dorr takes pride in his African heritage and enters into the acrimonious arena of argumentation with proslavery advocates, but he presents these as the frivolous musings of a dilettante. And he identifies himself multiply as "colored," "quadroon," "slave," "black," and as a "southern" gentleman. These contradictory racial interpellations or namings can be explained, in part, by the particularities of antebellum New Orleans as well as of Dorr's personal situation.

The facts about Dorr's life are scarce but can be pieced together from his enlistment and veteran's disability records. We know that Dorr was born a slave in 1827 or 1828 in New Orleans.[6] His owner was Cornelius Fellowes, a lawyer who, Dorr mentions, treated him all his life like a son.[7] Dorr was apparently light-skinned enough to pass for white.[8] For three years, from 1851 to 1854, Dorr traveled with his master around Europe and the Near East, Fellowes having promised Dorr his manumission upon return to the United States. When Fellowes reneged upon his promise, Dorr escaped from Louisiana to Ohio. It is not known whether his master attempted to hunt for him. No notice of a reward for Dorr appeared in either of the major New Orleans newspapers, the *Daily Picayune* or the *New Orleans Bee*, in 1854.

In Ohio he moved to Cleveland, where he decided to publish his account of his travels, based upon the diary he had kept. Dorr obviously had, or mustered up, the resources to have his book privately printed. *A Colored Man Round the World* was published in September 1858 and attracted enough attention to be reviewed immediately in all three major Cleveland newspapers— the *Cleveland Plain Dealer,* the *Daily Cleveland Herald,* and the *Cleveland Leader.* However, the *Anti-Slavery Bugle,* the only black newspaper published anywhere near the vicinity (Salem, Ohio) in 1858, includes no mention of it. The book was similarly ignored by the *National Anti-Slavery Standard.*

Although the city directories do not list Dorr in Cleveland at this time, he apparently lived in the area and made his living as a clerk.[9] The little information available about Dorr suggests a somewhat arrogant young man, proud of his erudition, and consciously affiliating himself with African-Americans. In May 1860, for instance, he arranged to deliver a lecture, "The Ballet Girls and Quadroon Ladies, and the Nobleman and Merchant Prince," at the popular Cleveland hall, the Melodeon. Again, notices of the lecture appeared in all the three major Cleveland newspapers. The talk was postponed due to a small audience, drawing the ire of Dorr, who wrote a letter to the editor of the *Cleveland Plain Dealer* lamenting the banality of intellectual life in the Western Reserve.[10] On August 26, 1862, in Cleveland, Dorr enlisted as a private in the Seventh Ohio Volunteer Infantry (O.V.I.), where he served till November 1863, when he was wounded in the head and shoulder at the battle of Ringgold in Georgia. He was discharged on August 15, 1864, in Cleveland.

For the next few years, Dorr's life seems to have been one of physical debility and legal wranglings. The wound on his jaw was painful and disfiguring, rendering him incapable of masticating solid foods, while the wound to his shoulder prevented full movement of his right arm. In short, as he declared in his Invalid Pension form, he was unable to perform any labor. In 1865, Dorr was pensioned at a rate of six dollars per month in Cleveland, his disability being declared temporary. By March 1867, however,

☞ "A COLORED MAN ROUND THE WORLD."—
A neat little volume with this title has just been
published in this city by the author, Mr. David
Dorr. The book is a graphic and racy sketch of
the author's travels in foreign lands—what he saw,
heard and experienced. The author claims no
special merit for it as a literary work, yet we think
he has succeeded in making an exceedingly
interesting work, and one which must command a
wide and ready sale. He indulges in no pompous
rhetoric, but jots down in a free-and-easy, every-
day style the incidents of his travels. He tells us
of what he saw and did in Liverpool, Paris, the
Netherlands, at Waterloo, in Ghent, Rome, Naples, Constantinople, Athens, Venice, Florence,
Cairo, on the Desert, at Jerusalem, Jerico and Damascus, &c., &c. The author was in Paris during
the coup-d'etat of Louis Napoleon, and gives us a
thrilling account of the scenes and sensations of
the time when "the fate of Paris, like a stormy
sea, was rocking to and fro." The author is a
Quadroon but would readily pass any where as a
white man (and an excellent white man, too,) but
he is still not ashamed to call himself "A Colored
Man Round the World." He dedicates his book
to his "Slave Mother." It is for sale at the book
stores.

Review of *A Colored Man Round the World.*
(*Cleveland Plain Dealer,* September 20, 1858, 3.)

Mr. Dorr's Lecture,

Mr. Dorr, an Octoroon gentleman who has "traveled," announced that he would speak on Saturday evening last in regard to "the Ballet Girls of Paris and Quadroon Ladies of the South," at the Melodeon. He went to an expense of $37, but only about two dozen persons were present. He concluded to postpone the lecture. He writes us a letter in which he says:

My lecture of "the Ballet Girls and Quadroon Ladies," I rehearsed at the Melodeon on Friday evening, before a Greek, Latin and French scholar, to his entire approbation. He had never heard any lecture *par excellence* of novelty and interest.

Now, my friends insist upon my getting a list of ladies and gentlemen to *call my lecture*. I said to them I was willing to put it off until the theater closed, and then appear again on my own expense, and if I did not get people to come and hear a *classical arrangement* of the various *silent intrigues* that are governing all classes of society, I would offer to the *gay people* of Cleveland a *Free Lecture*; and if I could not then get an audience, I would offer to pay them a *cent apiece* to come and hear me *explain* some things they had not met thousands of times to *rehash* My subject, Mr. Editor, is an original one, and for *God's* sake let us have something original on the Western Reserve.

Your obedient servant,   DORR.

Those wishing to hear "a classical arrangement" of the subjects upon which Mr. DORR proposes to speak, will govern themselves accordingly when he next announces his lecture.

Dorr's letter to the *Cleveland Plain Dealer*

Dorr's deteriorating health caused the examining surgeon to declare his disability "permanent and total" and his pension to be increased to fifteen dollars per month. Soon thereafter, Dorr moved back to New Orleans, where, in 1871, he applied for another increase in pension. By this time Dorr's five-foot, eight-inch frame had wasted away to 115 pounds, and he suffered from extreme exhaustion. He probably died in 1872 or shortly thereafter.[11]

As the preceding biography intimates, the particularities of Dorr's social position are especially complex: born a quadroon in New Orleans in the 1830s, raised as an educated slave, and writing in Cleveland in the 1850s. Before the 1850s, as Joel Williamson suggests, a black-white distinction based on versions of the one-drop rule—any person with a drop of black blood being black—was not the case in New Orleans. Instead, mulattoes constituted a special third category, analogous to categories in Latin America.[12] The more affluent of free mulattoes "lived very well—nearly on a par with their white neighbors, to whom they were tied by bonds of kinship and culture."[13] Some rose to wealth through planter status and the ownership of slaves. It was only in the 1850s, when long-running intolerance of miscegenation elsewhere began to exert pressure in the lower South, that mulattoes began to lose their special status, although they continued to be counted in their own racial category by the Bureau of the Census until 1920.[14]

Mulattoes in New Orleans, particularly free mulattoes, thus constituted a distinct third category that cannot be fully understood through the black-white binary. Henry Louis Gates's contention that all "black texts are 'mulattoes' with a two-toned heritage" is well taken but does not explain the dualistic cultural specificity under which texts like Dorr's might have been written.[15] We need to consider reading African-American texts outside the important, but not all-explanatory, black-white binary—in this case that of the antebellum mulatto identity in the lower South. It is probably the existence of a large number of sophisticated, wealthy,

free mulattoes in New Orleans, who were by law barred from interacting with the dark-skinned slaves, that helps explain Dorr's self-definition in the preface: *"though a quadroon,* [the author] is pleased to announce himself the 'Colored man around the world'" (emphasis added).[16] Although a slave in New Orleans, Dorr was obviously aware of the social distinctions between mulattoes and the dark-skinned "colored" slaves, with whom the former did not naturally and readily identify. And yet, one must remember, as John Blassingame points out, that free mulattoes had to "be respectful in the company of whites and to obtain the permission of the mayor when [they] left the city, held balls, or formed social and benevolent societies."[17] Dorr thus writes from particularly vexed sites of race and class. He writes as part of a privileged group as an educated quadroon boy growing up in New Orleans, yet a slave; the jottings about his journeys are done soon after the passage of the Fugitive Slave Law of 1850, when political pressures are working to deny privileges to anyone with a visible admixture of black blood and when free New Orleans mulattoes are visibly beginning to identify with their enslaved brethren; the book itself is published in Cleveland, where only the black-white distinction holds, and which is free of slavery and progressive, but where too, the free African-American community forcefully expresses its marginalization by calling its short-lived newspaper the *Aliened American.*

Dorr's very decision to write a travel narrative, rather than a narrative of his own life and escape, becomes more understandable in light of these complex racial positions. And because it is the only work he wrote, the choice of genre is fraught with cultural significance and embedded in questions of antebellum African-American racial identity. By his own admission, Dorr was a privileged slave, treated by his master as if he were his own son; he also obviously had some money because, like many New Orleans mulattoes, he considered himself "more than equaled in dignity and means" to his master (12). Nevertheless, Dorr found his position as a slave unbearable enough to make an escape, leaving behind his mother, who was still a slave, in Louisiana. Despite the tolerance of mulattoes in New Orleans, it is important to emphasize that for most whites, slaves were simply commodities, articles for sale. Advertisements for the mass sale of "negroes" appeared every day in the *Daily Picayune* in the 1840s and 1850s, alongside with advertisements for horses, coaches, and face cream.[18] There were also notices, though less frequent, for the sale of mulattoes.[19] And notices of rewards, ranging from ten dollars to the occasional three hundred or five hundred dollars, for runaway slaves appeared frequently in the *New Orleans Bee* and the *Daily Picayune* in the mid-1850s, just when Dorr escaped his master. One such notice is worth mentioning because it demonstrates the particular hostility felt by the slaveowner threatened in his authority by the light-skinned mulatto. The notice reads, "Thomas, a mulatto boy, light complexioned, blue-eyes, aged about 25 years; 5 feet 10 inches in height, knock-kneed, bent back, surly look, discontented air. It is presumed that he has left New Orleans, with the intention of passing for a white man."[20] Dorr, the escaped slave, however, made his racial affiliation very clear in Ohio. Although he could have easily passed for an educated white, or as the writer for the *Cleveland Herald* put it, "an excellent white man," he continued to interpellate himself as a quadroon.[21]

Thus Dorr's decision to write a travel narrative based on the diary he kept of his travels, instead of a narrative of his life as a slave and his subsequent escape, is an important assertion of self as well as an intervention into the idea that different constituencies read Anglo-American and African-American writing. Most escaped slaves who ventured to write and publish began with accounts of their lives as slaves. They wrote, as William L. Andrews suggests, about freedom as a goal of their lives, but their freedom as writers was curtailed, to an extent, by writing under the aegis of white abolitionists, who promoted narratives of suffering and deprivation (including intellectual deprivation).[22] Many fought to retain agency and resist the commodification of their lives. Yet Frederick Douglass, William Wells Brown, and Harriet Jacobs all wrote personal narratives that were authenticated by prominent abolitionists. Brown could go on to write novels, travel narratives, dramas, and historical works only after he had published *Narrative of William Wells Brown, a Fugitive Slave,* in 1847.

This is not to suggest that accounts of slavery were not important to escaped slaves. The sheer volume of such narratives belies such an idea. Still, it is important to remember that northern white readers and abolitionist sponsors were prepared to accept only a certain type of blackness as "authentic" from former slaves, a blackness dependent upon a black-white binary. African-American writers were therefore constrained to perform narratives of suffering, humility, and perseverance, even as they rebelled against these constraints. Douglass's later autobiographies, *My Bondage and My Freedom* (1855) and *Life and Times of Frederick Douglass* (1881), increasingly stressed his autonomy and his role as a public figure. Instead of white abolitionist authentication, the second autobiography included an introduction by Dr. J. McCune Smith, a prominent African-American physician. Yet even if their texts confounded the expectations of white abolitionists, most antebellum African-American autobiographical narratives included overt declarations of racial uplift. Their rhetorical purposes included evoking the sympathy, righteous anger, and call to action from their readers.[23]

Dorr's personal situation obviously differed from that of most escaped slaves. He had the means to publish his own book without the help of white abolitionist sponsors. He organized his 1860 lecture at the Melodeon at the personal expense of thirty-seven dollars, more than six months' worth of the pension he would receive in 1865. Yet, in a very real, personal sense, Dorr's circumstances were similar to that of other escaped slaves. In order to gain his freedom by fleeing to the North, Dorr was forced to lose contact with his mother, a fact poignantly recorded in his book's dedication "To My Slave Mother." Dorr's use of the structure of genteel travel narratives for his book thus boldly questions the idea of a singular racial identity constructed solely through dualistic racial oppositions and defined by a constant, overt polemic against racial oppression. Instead, Dorr posits a mulatto selfhood perfectly comfortable being positioned as genteel Anglo *and,* simultaneously, identifiably African-American, the kind of mulatto identity whites in the lower South had started to fear and loathe. Or, within the dualistic parameters of Cleveland, one could say that Dorr performs whiteness in order to better create a subversive form of blackness, one that questions the working-class ideological affiliations of antebellum black culture, but one that also indicts the hierarchies of the slaveholding society.[24] Ultimately, Dorr's book attests to the heterogeneous modes of antebellum African-American protest writing.

It would, of course, be a historical oversimplification to think of antebellum African-American texts as just transparent reflections of a dogmatic ideological purpose. Indeed, as many critics have suggested, African-American texts are constituted by different kinds of dual articulations. From Houston Baker's delineation of the contradictory construction of African-American identities caught within black and white worlds, to Sterling Stuckey's exposition of black verbal forms as ways of concealing meaning and deceiving whites, to Henry Louis Gates's positioning of the trickster as a central figure in African-American writing, it has long been clear that even the earliest of these texts were cunningly and complexly constructed in order to appeal to or appease a white readership.[25] Not surprisingly, the most revisited critical sites within these texts are those that position themselves polemically and displace racial hierarchies. Two such instances are Douglass's reclamation of manhood by striking his master and Harriet Jacobs's decision to have an affair with a white man in order to elude the lasciviousness of her master. Dorr's text does not explicitly invite attention to such moments because the aesthetic apparatus of comfortable travel writing is so complete. Hegel uses the term *Dasein* to refer to the surface appearance of rest in a text or social formation beneath which is a restlessness we can see only when we crack the surface. In *A Colored Man Round the World,* genteel travel writing, and all the ideologies it assumes, is the apparent *Dasein,* one that marks the speaker as putatively "white." But this *Dasein,* this assumption of white forms, a sort of metaphoric whiteface, is at once a violent conjunction of contradictions and an audacious appropriation almost unparalleled in antebellum African-American writing.

NINETEENTH-CENTURY ANGLO-AMERICAN AND AFRICAN-AMERICAN TRAVEL WRITING

In order to better understand Dorr's use and manipulation of the forms of Anglo-American travel writing, we need to take a brief look at travel writing as a genre used by both Anglo-Americans and African-Americans. Nineteenth-century Americans were voracious consumers of travel literature. Between 1800 and 1868 alone, some seven hundred books of travel were published.[26] The majority of these were about travel to Europe, but after the introduction of steam packets in the 1830s, many Americans chose Oriental destinations, the most popular being Egypt and the Holy Lands. The forms of Anglo-American travel writing were partly molded by these destinations.

For most Anglo-Americans, traveling to Europe was a ritual of cultural affirmation and affiliation.[27] Here, the writings of Pierre Bourdieu, the French sociologist, are helpful in thinking about the relationship between class and culture that is integral to Dorr's text. Writing about art and culture, as Anglo-American travelers to Europe did, would be evidence of an accumulation of cultural capital that "can only be acquired by means of a sort of withdrawal from economic necessity."[28] This acquisition of culture favors "an enchanted experience of culture" predicated on forgetting the economic and social means of acquiring it.[29] Acquisition of European cultural capital and the writing about enchantment with this culture was thus preeminently a class privilege marking aristocratic heredity and taste and moral and civic virtue, rather than economic means alone. In antebellum America, the acquisition of this cultural capital and the status it conferred was very largely a genteel Anglo privilege, although in the lower South it could, to an extent, also be a mulatto privilege.

For the already elite, such as Henry Adams or James Fenimore Cooper, the contact with European history, art, and society, was a confirmation of their own status as possessors of this cultural capital through reading, schooling, and social contact. For middle-class or poor writers like Bayard Taylor, it was an opportunity to acquire genteel status through firsthand contact with Old World culture. Frederick Douglass rightly saw Anglo travel to Europe as the supreme form access to manners and class. Going to Britain was what "young American gentlemen" did "to increase their stock of knowledge, to seek pleasure, to have their rough, democratic manners softened by contact with English aristocratic refinement."[30] Manners, morals, and class were complexly interlinked. The situation for African-Americans, he made clear, was very different. Thus, no matter what their economic status, Anglo-American travel writers to Europe wrote with a tone of gentility and assumed a literariness that marked them as refined, different from their more provincial brethren at home. And they wrote with appropriate respect for the artifacts of European culture. Christopher Mulvey explains that

> the most pervasive fiction constructed by the nineteenth-century travel writer was that of the gentility of the writer and reader. Literary decorum demanded that an author assume a

genteel voice in order to address society. . . . The writer-travellers were therefore obliged to adopt a tone of voice which suggested very often that they were of higher social standing than that to which their actual social incomes or birth might otherwise entitle them.[31]

This is not to suggest that Anglo-American travel writers to Europe wrote only about art and monuments. Nathaniel Parker Willis, for instance, commented on the poverty of the working classes, but these comments were presented as digressions from the predominant objective of writing about culture.[32] And the image he presented to the public was that of the gentleman of leisure who wrote "in a crimson-curtained parlour strewn with ottomans and 'lap-me-delightfullys.'"[33] Similarly, Bayard Taylor, who actually had to approach numerous newspapers and journals to have his passage financed, made sure that his travel writing reflected a genteel, inherited cultural capital that European history and art confirmed. Every step in Westminster Abbey, for instance, recalls for Taylor "some mind linked with the associations of my childhood";[34] the castles and towns along the Rhine evoke memories: "Every place was familiar to me in memory, and they seemed like friends I had long communed with in spirit and now met face to face."[35] This kind of travel writing about Europe thus interpellated the traveler as cultivated, leisured, and free from necessity—in other words, genteel and Anglo.

Anglo-Americans traveling to the "Orient," on the other hand, had little cultural anxiety. Here they simply assumed their roles as part of an imperial Western culture (indeed for many, the United States was the new empire) and wrote confidently from this superior position about the backward and passive, though exotic, Orient.[36] George William Curtis's *The Howadji in Syria* (1852), begins, for instance, with exotic images of "acacia groves," "costumes whose picturesqueness is poetry," and the harems of the pashas.[37] "Oriental" civilization, Curtis suggests, is a chimera of the past: "The poets at the cafes tell the old tales. The splendors of the caliphat flash, a boreal brilliance, over an unreal past. . . . Thus oriental life is an echo and a ghost."[38] In both cases, however, Anglo-American writers projected themselves into a European cultural tradition, citing previous travelers and historians, admitting what William Stowe calls "their cultural belatedness."[39] For the most, then, Anglo-American travel writing did not seek to challenge or resist the conception of high culture in America.

African-American travel writers, on the other hand, wrote from a very different sense of purpose. During the antebellum period, African-American travel writers were either escaped or freed slaves or freeborn. Travel writing, through geographic displacement, offered these writers complex identity formations. As Stowe suggests, William Wells Brown's travel narrative allowed him to claim a stake in the genteel Anglo-European tradition through which he then expounded his ideas on racial equality.[40] Gentility, for Brown, became a vehicle serving the major purpose of promoting racial justice. Thus no matter what roles they assumed, a major rhetorical purpose of the writings of African-Americans was to awaken their countrymen to the unjust and uncivilized degradation faced not only by slaves in the South, but by blacks everywhere in the United States. African-Americans traveling to Europe repeatedly testified to the sense of empowerment they felt at being treated without contempt in Europe. It was almost the birth of a new identity. At the end of chapter 1 of his travelogue, *The American Fugitive in Europe* (1855), William Wells Brown writes about this creation of a new sense of self thus:

> No person of my complexion can visit this country without being struck with the marked difference between the English and the Americans. The prejudice which I have experienced on all and every occasion in the United States, and to some extent on board the Canada, vanished as soon as I set foot on

the soil of Britain. In America I had been bought and sold as a slave in the Southern States. In the so-called Free States, I had been treated as one to occupy an inferior position. . . . But no sooner was I on British soil, than I was recognized as a man, and an equal. The very dogs in the streets appeared conscious of my manhood.[41]

As the last sentence suggests, Britain allows Brown to construct a patriarchal (manly) selfhood inaccessible to him in America. In the expanded and revised 1892 version of his autobiography, *Life and Times of Frederick Douglass,* Douglass similarly contrasted the effects of racial distinctions in Britain and the United States: "Instead of a democratic government, I am under a monarchical government. . . . I breathe, and lo! the chattel becomes a man!"[42] In her observations on Russia, Nancy Prince reported the comparative lack of color prejudice there.[43] Julia Griffiths's "Letters From The Old World" likewise focused on the formation and expansion of antislavery societies in England.[44] Similarly, Mary Ann Shadd Cary, in her descriptions of Canada, focused on Canada as an agricultural emigration territory for African-Americans. The possible attraction to the posture of the genteel Anglo traveler did not overshadow their consciousness of writing as marginalized racial subjects.[45]

A number of African-Americans also wrote accounts of their travels to Africa and the Caribbean. Unlike Anglo-American narratives, however, the purpose of these accounts was not to titillate the reader with exoticism or to document the depravities of savage Africans, but to examine the issue of African-American emigration and to offer evidence of the salubrious effects of self-government. Nancy Prince's representations of Jamaicans, for instance, stridently counter stereotypes of them as shiftless people not fit for independence.[46] Dennis Harris's *A Summer on the Borders of the Caribbean Sea* (1860) includes a preface by the popular travel writer George William Curtis, but its concern is with the future of African-Americans. Harris's travelogue painstakingly proves the desirability of African-American colonies in Central America and Haiti, including in the proof laudatory biographies of Toussaint L'Ouverture and discussion of the effects of black empowerment in Jamaica. Similarly, concerns about the viability of wholesale African-American emigration to Liberia motivated African-American writing about the country, no matter what the position taken. Thus William Nesbit, who saw the project as a wholesale deceit, intended to simply get rid of African-Americans, depicted Liberia as a land of darkness in *Four Months in Liberia;* on the other hand, Rev. Samuel Williams, in *Four Years in Liberia,* represented emigration as a promise and praised both the conversion of natives in Liberia as well as the mode of government.

Despite variations among the nearly seven hundred antebellum travel narratives, they are characterized by an important distinction between Anglo-American and African-American works. While Anglo-American works were accounts of cultural initiation written with a sense of participation in, or desire to participate in, a Europeanized culture, African-American travel works were closely tied with questions of black racial difference and slavery, even if, like Robert Campbell's *A Pilgrimage to My Motherland* (1861), they also provided conventional accounts of peoples and cultures or included aspirations to Anglo gentility.[47] Most importantly, African-Americans critiqued the denial of their rights by disaffiliation with American citizenship. "The meanest thing I have been obliged to do, and the greatest sin I have committed," wrote Dennis Harris, "has been the registering my name as an American citizen."[48] Given the divergent social functions of Anglo-American and African-American travel narratives, the former serving as cultural enhancement and the latter furthering the amelioration of the race, Dorr's narrative stands as a unique literary creation. It is probably Dorr's distance from traditional forms of antebellum African-American writing that has led to his virtual omission from bibliographies or critical works on African-American literature, much like Harriet Wilson.[49] Monroe N. Work's *A Bibliography of the Negro in Africa and America* (1928) makes no mention of Dorr; nor does Benjamin Brawley's *Early Negro American Writers* (1935). He is mentioned in Geraldine O. Matthews's massive compilation *Black American Writers, 1773–1949: A Bibliography and Union List,* but in the history section rather than the literature section. In Dorothy W. Campbell's *Index to Black American Writers in Collective Biographies* (1983), Dorr is again erased. William Andrews in *To Tell a Free Story* mentions Dorr's work briefly in a footnote. My own discovery of Dorr came through Fuad Sha'ban's reading of *A Colored Man Round the World* in *Islam and Arabs in Early American Thought* (1991).[50]

The neglect of Dorr's text is probably a result of his decision to write his narrative through a complete and wholesale usage of genteel Anglo forms. *A Colored Man Round the World* appropriates the forms and structures of Anglo-American travel writing so completely that what we have is a superb case of literary doublespeak: the blackest of texts in whiteface. Dorr's positioning of racial identity can usefully be thought of as a deliberate "performance," not simply aspiring to whiteness (a position critiqued by Fannon in *Black Skin, White Masks*) but using what we might call "whiteface," a deliberate donning of whiteness that, unlike blackface, was not culturally sanctioned.[51] Dorr presents his enchantment of European culture through and despite his pride in his African ancestry; he displays an Anglo gentility but also demonstrates the lack of class of rich southern whites, thus questioning a major assumption of white identity in the antebellum South; and he rewrites relations of power during slavery by making his master an object. On another level, and most evidently, Dorr clearly writes of himself as a leisured traveler, a position that was overwhelmingly white.

Dorr's undermining of racial hierarchies begins in what seems the most visibly raced parts of the text—the dedication and the preface. Here we particularly note Dorr's determination to create a new voice for himself. Dorr eschews all forms of authentication—whether those of abolitionists or other Anglo travel writers. It is important here to keep in mind the raced nature of conventions of authorship. William Charvat's enormously influential papers have shown the pervasiveness of the "gentleman-amateur" convention of anonymous authorship till the 1820s, its vestiges continuing in some cases till the 1840s and 1850s.[52] But for African-American writers, precisely the opposite was true. Anonymous authorship meant white authorship because for whites, literacy could simply be assumed. On the other hand, an anonymously authored work could not be presumed to be black. African-American literacy and authorship, particularly that of former slaves, had to be laboriously authenticated through prefaces, introductions, and testimonials.

Travel writing as a genre allowed writers a little more freedom than did personal narratives, but many African-American travel narratives still included proofs of expertise. William Nesbit's *Four Months in Liberia* includes an introduction by Martin Delaney, while Robert Campbell announces his numerous official designations on the title page of his book, *A Pilgrimage to My Motherland:* "One of the Commissioners of the Niger Valley Exploring Party; late in charge of the Scientific Department for Colored Youth, Philadelphia; and Member of the International Statistical Congress, London." *A Colored Man Round the World* disrupts these conventions in complex ways. The book begins without authentication, but simply with a personal dedication to his mother and with Dorr's preface. As if in the genteel, Anglo tradition, Dorr's name appears nowhere on the title page. Instead, the book is presented as authored "by a Quadroon." Such a complication of authorship suggests Dorr's difference from both the assumed (Anglo) norm of anonymous authorship and the laboriously achieved subjecthood of former slaves. The designation of the book as written "by a Quadroon" also emphasizes the power of racial definition and of Dorr's own raced identity.

In the dedication and preface, antislavery sentiments and questions of African racial pride obviously predominate, but Dorr undermines racial hierarchies even more resolutely by an almost audacious cultural appropriation. The book begins with a dedication directed to his slave mother from whom the author is separated; as such, it testifies eloquently to the cruel breakup of the family under the slave system, as did Douglass's account in his *Narrative* and Jacobs's rendition of her enforced separation from her children while in hiding in *Incidents in the Life of a Slave Girl.* The author is denied all information about the whereabouts of his mother. But at the same time he laments this lack of information, he situates his mother both as Revolutionary American and as slave: "Mother! wherever thou art, whether in Heaven or a lesser world; or whether around the freedom Base of a Bunker Hill, or only at the lowest savannah of American Slavery . . ." The dedication parallels abolitionist and revolutionary histories and appropriates the bastions of Anglo history for African-Americans. Written in the aftermath of the *Dred Scott* decision that denied citizenship to African-Americans, such a parallel is particularly empowering.

A similar kind of audacious appropriation and distorted mirroring is evident in the preface. Although only in his twenties when he traveled, having learned to read despite laws mandating slave illiteracy, Dorr positions himself with ease as a scholar. Like many learned African-Americans of his time, Dorr invokes racial pride by linking his ancestry with ancient Egyptian civilization. Egyptology had created considerable consternation for both phrenologists and theorists of racial classification because of the non-Caucasian features of Egyptian monuments like the Sphinx and the existence of people with negroid-African features in many of the carvings and parchments of Egyptian antiquity. While proslavery anthropologists strove to demonstrate the lowly status of black peoples in Egypt, prominent African-Americans like Frederick Douglass, Henry Highland Garnet, and later Pauline Hopkins, used Egyptology to validate the idea of Africans being the originators of civilization.[53] Dorr similarly lauds black Egyptians as his "ancestors": "Well, who were the Egyptians? Ask Homer if their lips were not thick, their hair curly, their feet flat and their skin black" (11). Yet he ends the preface with the appropriation of a clearly imperialist cultural identity. He has decided, he says, to escape his master and flee "westward, where the 'star of empire takes its way'" (12). By invoking George Berkeley's famous line, "Westward the course of Empire takes its way," which was echoed by numerous nineteenth-century politicians in order to legitimize expansionism, Dorr ironically conflates the forced flight of the fugitive slave with the imperial ventures of the United States. Coming at a crucial juncture in the text, just before the beginning of Dorr's travel narrative, this conflation puts under question the very freedom of travel that the narrative, as whiteface, celebrates.

In the dedication and preface, Dorr constitutes himself as a subject within the text of slavery, but in the rest of the text, for nearly two hundred pages, he interpellates himself as an "American" ready to roam the world, as genteel traveler instructing his readers, and as gentleman being waited on by maids and lackeys. How, then, do we as readers reconcile these opposed constructions of the author as unfree and free? William W. Stowe suggests that Dorr, like William Wells Brown, uses his narrative for empowerment: "The most remarkable feature of Dorr's text is its counterfactual narrative persona. . . . He uses travel writing as a dry run for freedom, a vehicle for fantasy, a way to dream what it might be like to be free, to imagine himself into an equal relationship with everyone he meets."[54] Dorr himself is acutely conscious of the limits placed on his subjectivity through his interpellation as a slave and his textual transgression of that interpellation. In the opening paragraph of chapter 14, "The Secrets of a

Paris Life, and Who Knows Them," Dorr provides the reader
with a key to reading his text: "Reader, can a man dream with his
eyes open? or can a man see with them shut? . . . Then let me
dream of what I saw" (87). For the remainder of the chapter,
Dorr intentionally offers a confusing set of textual cues so that
we are never quite sure how, where, or when the dream portions
can be separated from the travel narrative proper. This imagina-
tive freedom is not simply personal but rather imbued with questions of race, power, and authority. *Traveler,* in the Anglo sense,
was a status not allowed slaves or servants. "In the dominant dis-
courses of travel," as James Clifford points out, "a non-white
person cannot figure as a heroic explorer, aesthetic interpreter,
or scientific authority."[55] However, through the display of cultural capital, a privilege generally allowed only leisured white
Americans, Dorr brings together, and thus undermines, what the
dominant culture had (even in the lower South in the 1850s)
increasingly come to see as absolute oppositions: genteel and
African-American; and more significantly, learned and slave.

Dorr's deliberate performance of whiteface creates a racial
and narrative instability that, in turn, destabilizes the reader's
racial and cultural assumptions. It is no wonder that contemporary reviewers of *A Colored Man* felt uncomfortable affixing a
particular racial identity to Dorr. Cleveland, like many progressive northern cities in the antebellum era, offered simultaneous
racial enlightenment and stereotypical racial division. All the
major Cleveland newspapers, for instance, expressed outrage at
the attempted returning of fugitive slaves in the Oberlin rescue
case; yet, blackface minstrel shows such as the Morris Brothers
and Hooley & Campbell's were enthusiastically advertised as
well.[56] Understandably, area readers of *A Colored Man Round
the World* were confused about Dorr's racial identity. For the
reviewer of the *Daily Cleveland Herald,* Dorr was only putatively black. The reviewer wrote, "This is a book of 192 pages
and is the journey of a colored man—if a Quadroon comes un-

der that title."[57] The comments of the reviewer for the *Cleveland Plain Dealer* reveal how Dorr's performance works to shatter the idea of a stable racial identity. Unable to interpellate the author in a single manner, the reviewer positions Dorr at the interstices of three raced categories: "white" as norm, "colored" as other, and "quadroon" as mixed. "The author is a Quadroon but would readily pass any where as a white man (and an excellent white man, too,) but he is still not ashamed to call himself 'A Colored Man Round the World.'"[58] Empowerment, Dorr suggests, comes from destabilizing the dualistic hierarchies on which the dominant culture's ideologies rest. As a quadroon from New Orleans, Dorr was uniquely positioned to attempt such a destabilization.

Perhaps the most transgressive effects of Dorr's assumption of Anglo-American gentility and culture is in Dorr's representation of his master, Cornelius Fellowes, and of other southern white men. One of the most fascinating features of Dorr's narrative is the fact that the term *master* is never used.[59] In most of his travels, carousings, and occasional difficulties with European manners, Dorr simply ignores his master, Cornelius Fellowes. But when he does introduce him in the narrative and devotes an entire chapter to him entitled "Col. Fellowes Learning Dutch," Fellowes appears as an object to be looked at and assessed, much like a slave on the auction block: "He is rather more than a medium size man, and straight as an exclamation point, with handsome limbs" (61). For the rest of the chapter, Dorr holds Fellowes up to ridicule and contempt as he scoffs at the latter's lack of sophistication and poor judgment. Fellowes's vulgar amusement over beggars running after the coins he throws ends up, for instance, making him a victim of beggars who pull at his clothes when he has no more money. Dorr writes, "Mr. Fellowes showed tokens of fear, and he hallowed out, 'Lacquey, why don't you take a stick and beat them off, don't you see they are robbing me?'" (68). By inverting racial hierarchies through the lens of taste and class, Dorr questions the cultural assumptions that link race, class, and culture in the antebellum United States.

In the rest of the text, Dorr extends his genteel disgust to the most powerful within the racial hierarchies of antebellum America: southern white men. The southerner's very performance of southernness signifies his want of class. As the narrator observes in a public hall in Paris, "not one gentleman had his foot on the table, except an American quietly seated in one corner in profound soliloquy. He was chewing tobacco. I didn't stop to see where he spit, for fear he might claim nationality" (40). It is this kind of glorification in an upper-class status that marks Dorr's text as fundamentally different from that of other antebellum African-American travel writers. While most African-Americans harshly criticized their white countrymen for their want of morality, their complicity with slavery or racial oppression, Dorr expends great narrative energy criticizing them for their want of class. Cultural capital, a traditionally Anglo-American commodity, and gentility, the expression of Anglo-American class and virtue, become the issues here.

Like Anglo-American travel writers, Dorr presents his encounter with European history and culture as a belated one, as cultural inheritance. When Dorr evaluates Zurich as "the prettiest city in Switzerland," for instance, he does so in the spirit of correction, in light of Byron's praise of Geneva (47). In Frankfurt, the narrator makes the appropriate literary pilgrimage to Goethe's house, while in Heidelberg he invokes the novels *The Castles of Heidelberg* and *Erhreinstein.* In the manner of traditional Anglo-American travel narratives, Dorr also pays appropriate homage to the contemporary and historical architectural feats of Europe, including the Crystal Palace in London, Notre Dame in Paris, and St. Peter's Church in Rome. Dorr does not simply describe Roman ruins but also provides the reader a history of emperors and senators. Writing thus becomes the occasion to display scholarship and learning. Dorr also uses the formal properties of his text to signify his cultural capital. *A Colored Man Round the World* is filled with references to literary figures such as Shakespeare, Byron, Shelley, and Goethe, and historians such as Plutarch. And as a final sign of culture, Dorr uses his New Orleans background advantageously by using French words and phrases at various points in the narrative.

A *Colored Man Round the World* also invites us to examine the writer's construction of a gender identity in relation to racial construction. Like other Anglo-American travel writers, particularly those traveling to the Orient, Dorr uses his narrative to enact a traditional masculinity. The idea of the Orient being figured as woman, against which a Westerner could define his masculinity, as has been well articulated by Edward Said.[60] Anglo-American travel writers such as George William Curtis and Nathaniel Parker Willis routinely wrote about their fascination with harems, Oriental women, and an exotic, feminized culture. As if in whiteface, Dorr continues to write within this Anglo-American Orientalist tradition. In Turkey, the fragile, diminutive, inactive women serve as a metonym for a supine "Orient" against which the author defines his masculinity: "I would have given five pds to lift her veil; I know she was pretty, her voice was so fluty, and her hands so delicate, and her feet so small, and her dress so gauzy; she was like an eel" (123). Oriental women might be unreal and shadowy, but women await Dorr everywhere in the text. The narrator's position throughout the text is that of empowered male. The "colored man" whose ownership of his own body was highly contingent in the United States, and who was denied the privileges of patriarchy within the slave system, becomes a hero with constant access to the European maids that wait on him in hotels and the Oriental women waiting to be unveiled. In fact, Dorr seems quite self-conscious of his role as traveling rake: "A man is a good deal like a dog in some particulars. . . . as soon as he sees his sexual mate, his attention is manifested in the twinkling of an eye" (15). Despite the critique, however, the assumption of the role of empowered male is both undeni-

able and racially significant. Exploiting the patriarchal impera-
tives of Orientalism allows Dorr to affirm his selfhood in a culture that denied him legitimacy both as subject of a nation and
as male subject. Claiming manhood was crucial in questioning
the hierarchies of the slave system even though the models for
this manhood were white and imperial. Whiteface performance
thus problematically reinscribes, even as it critiques, both
Orientalism and a dominant masculinity.

Dorr's assumption of the cultural capital and the power inherent in the forms of the Anglo-American travel narrative thus allows him access to a white readership that was more comfortable
seeing his text as white than as whiteface or mulatto. But Dorr
does not simply attempt to "pass"; rather, his whiteface performance calls attention to the right of African-Americans to cultural capital. The very title of his book makes it clear that Dorr
wishes to be thought of as "colored"; and, as we have seen, he
voices his affinity with the culture of Africa and with the black
men he meets during his journeys. Dorr's text attests powerfully
to the heterogeneity of antebellum African-American literature
and to the heterogeneity of slave experiences. We can think of
Dorr's use of Anglo travel-writing forms as particularly well suited
to the manner in which he wishes to mediate the experience of
slavery—not as a suffering victim, but as privileged gentleman,
the very use of the status signifying his determination to free
himself of his slave condition.

Dorr thus critiques American slavery and racial oppression,
not so much through expostulatory polemic as through genteel
understatement, humor, and irony. While marveling at the world's
fair in London, for instance, he mocks the uncouth *manners* and
stupidity of the South Carolinian who would have exhibited his
slaves as part of the American exhibit. His stupidity, Dorr points
out, lies in his not realizing that the slaves would surely consider
escape. The immorality of slaveowning is not explicitly addressed,
but implicitly understood. Read in the context of Dorr's own sta-

tus as slave traveling with his master, it is also a poignant allegory of his own position as slave exhibit. It is in a similar manner that we can read the numerous references to African-Americans and Africans in Europe and the Near East: Mr. Cordevoille, the respected quadroon from New Orleans, and Frank Parish, who towers over the sultan of Turkey.

Dorr concludes his narrative by affirming his solidarity with people of African heritage even though he maintains the Anglo stance of the leisured traveler. Dorr enters into the heated debate between monogenists who believed in a single story of human creation beginning with Adam and Eve, and polygenists, who argued for multiple versions of creation. Supporters of monogenesis argued for the unity of human beings, delineated in the story of creation in Genesis. Polygenists, on the other hand, could not accept the idea of the fundamental unity of races and looked to scientific theories in order to support their beliefs about the complete and absolute separation of Caucasian and African races. Samuel George Morton's *Crania Americana,* published in the United States in 1839, provided proslavery apologists ammunition for supporting slavery on the grounds of moral differences among races. Dorr, like Frederick Douglass, whom he may have heard speaking about the subject, obviously followed these debates keenly and was aware of the large audience for them.[61] He chooses to conclude his narrative by addressing these readers and arguing for the inherent reasonableness of monogenesis or "the doctrine of the unity of man" (192). In supporting monogenesis, Dorr aligns himself with major African-American publications such as the *National Anti-Slavery Standard* and the *Anglo-African Magazine* that in the 1850s often published articles questioning the ethics of polygenists.

Yet even while questioning theories of racial supremacy, Dorr maintains the stance of the cultured traveler. It is as a leisured and cultured gentleman that Dorr wishes to position himself, a position from which he demands recognition, not angrily or heatedly, but with cool presumption. That is why he situates what could, in the writings of someone like David Walker, be read as radical and revolutionary, as simply the exhortations of youth: "When you hear *can't*, laugh at it; when they tell you *not in your time,* pity them; and when they tell you *surrounding circumstances alter cases,* in manliness scorn them" (191–92). But to read them as simply the musings of a youthful dandy, without relevance to antebellum African-American experience, is to deny the heterogeneity of African-American voices and the ability of culturally hybridized writers such as Dorr to radically subvert Western forms.

Reading Dorr today reminds us of the multiplicity of African-American experiences, even under slavery, and the different forms taken by antebellum African-American writing. In a period when blackface was tolerated and enjoyed as a means of emphasizing stereotypes of African-Americans, Dorr's text asks us what it means to appropriate whiteface but not "pass." Most importantly, *A Colored Man Round the World* fundamentally questions the idea of an accepted "type" of ethnic literature. At a time when ethnic authenticity and identity are being problematized in disciplines as diverse as history, anthropology, sociology, and literary studies, Dorr's text invites us to explore the complexity of these issues, both in the nineteenth century and today.

NOTES

1. *Dred Scott v. Sanford, United States Reports,* vol. 60, 393, 395.

2. Mary Louise Pratt, *Imperial Eyes: Travel Writing and Transculturation* (New York: Routledge, 1992), 5.

3. My use of "class" in this essay refers to a particular lifestyle in addition to economic distinction. The idea of what constituted antebellum white identity (regional or otherwise) has been the subject of much recent scholarship. The relevant aspect here is that the normalized idea

of white identity separated itself from the lives and habits of poor whites who were often likened to African-Americans. See especially Shelley Fisher Fishkin, *Was Huck Black?* (New York: Oxford University Press, 1993), 28.

4. Pierre Bourdieu explains the acquisition of various forms of cultural capital—manners, the aesthetic disposition—as dependent upon class. "Legitimate manners," writes Bourdieu, "owe their value to the fact that they manifest the rarest conditions of acquisition, that is, a social power over time that is tacitly recognized as the supreme excellence: to possess things from the past, i.e., accumulated, crystallized history, aristocratic names and titles, chateaux or 'stately homes,' paintings and collections . . . is to master time . . . by inheritance or through dispositions which, like the taste for old things, are likewise only acquired with time and applied by those who can take their time. Pierre Bourdieu, *Distinction: A Social Critique of the Judgement of Taste,* Trans. Richard Nice (Cambridge: Harvard University Press, 1984), 71–72.

5. See Bourdieu, *Distinction,* 175.

6. Because birth certificates were not issued for slaves in Louisiana, no birth record is available for Dorr. The *Official Roster of the Soldiers of the State of Ohio in the War of the Rebellion, 1861–1866,* vol. 2 (Cincinnati: Wilstach, Baldwin, 1886), 234, lists Dorr's age as twenty-seven at the time of enlistment (1862), but in his September 1871 application for the increase of invalid pension Dorr lists his age as 43, which would put his year of birth at 1828. The latter is probably more accurate because it is a record of what Dorr stated. An Examining Surgeon's Certificate, dated June 1872 lists Dorr as being 45, which would put his date of birth at 1827. Dorr's Certificate of Disability for Discharge lists his place of birth as New Orleans.

7. The New Orleans city directories for the 1840s and 1850s show no listing for Cornelius Fellowes as the owner of a law firm at the address Dorr lists in his book. However, the directories do list Felloweses as the proprietors of a firm of commission merchants (1846, 1849, 1850) and of cotton factors and commission merchants (1854, 1855, 1858).

8. A review of Dorr's book in the *Cleveland Plain Dealer* mentions that "the author is a Quadroon but would readily pass any where as a white man" (September 20, 1858, 3).

9. Dorr's Certificate of Disability for Discharge lists his occupation at the time of enlistment as a clerk.

10. *Cleveland Plain Dealer,* May 22, 1860, 3.

11. Dorr's last application for an increase of pension is dated August 1872. Given his failing health and the fact that the certificate for the increase of pension dated two months later has "dead" inscribed on it (though in a different hand), we can assume that Dorr died soon after. There are several discrepancies, however, in the war records pertaining to Dorr. Dorr's regiment, the Seventh O.V.I., acquired local and regional fame because of their annual reunions, encampments, and their publication, the *Rooster Record.* Dorr obviously did not participate in any of these reunions that were held in Cleveland but is shown to be receiving a pension in 1892. Because of the intensity of his wounds and the descriptions of his physical state in the pension records, as well as the fact that the pension records end in 1872, it is highly unlikely that Dorr was alive in 1892 as the *Rooster Record* suggests.

12. For an analysis of hybrid racial categories in Latin America see Garcia Nestor Canclini, *Hybrid Cultures: Strategies for Entering and Leaving Modernity,* trans. Christopher L. Chiappari and Silvia L. Lopez (Minneapolis: University of Minnesota Press, 1995).

13. Joel Williamson, *New People: Miscegenation and Mulattoes in the United States* (Baton Rouge: Louisiana State University Press, 1995), 14–15.

14. Williamson, *New People,* 3, 114.

15. Henry Louis Gates, *The Signifying Monkey: A Theory of African-American Literary Criticism* (New York: Oxford University Press, 1988), xxiii.

16. See John Blassingame, *Black New Orleans, 1860–1880* (Chicago: University of Chicago Press, 1973), 21.

17. Blassingame, *Black New Orleans,* 15. Blassingame does not pay much attention to the special status of mulattoes but points out that in New Orleans "a mulatto was generally a free man (77 percent of the free Negroes in 1860 were mulattoes)" (21).

18. The mid-1850s seem to have been a period of increased wholesale slave auctions. In January and February 1854, it was common for there to be two to three hundred slaves advertised for sale in a single day. The *Daily Picayune* for February 6, 1854, advertised 650 slaves for sale.

19. The January 21, 1854, *Daily Picayune,* for instance, advertised "A superior mulatto boy, 13 years age, acclimated, speaks French and English; fully guaranteed" (2).

20. *New Orleans Bee,* October 26, 1854, 3.

21. *Cleveland Plain Dealer,* September 20, 1858, 3.

22. William L. Andrews in his landmark *To Tell a Free Story: The First Century of Afro-American Autobiography, 1760–1865* (Urbana: University of Illinois Press, 1988), writes that early African-American autobiographies "'tell a free story' as well as talk about freedom as a theme and goal of life." These autobiographers demonstrate that "they regard the writing of autobiography as in some ways uniquely self-liberating" (xi).

23. Arlene A. Elder argues that similar purposes guide even early African-American fiction: "The overriding concern of most of the novelists was to show the 'true' nature of Blacks and to reveal the actual conditions of their lives. The writers wished to inspire pride and determination in African-Americans and to arouse understanding, sympathy, and a desire for political reform in their white audience" (*The "Hindered Hand": Cultural Implications of Early African-American Fiction* [Westport, Conn.: Greenwood Press, 1978], xiii).

24. Recently, there has been a lot of interesting work on the intersections of race and class. Shelley Fisher Fishkin's argument about Huck's blackness, mentioned earlier, relies on Blankenship's lower-class status. The assumed though unstated argument is that African-American culture could only have lower class affiliations (*Was Huck Black?* 28). Carla Peterson, however, makes a convincing argument for the black racial affiliations of antebellum middle-class free African-Americans. Using Fanon's argument about the estrangement of the "revolutionary elite" from the masses under conditions of colonization, Peterson argues that "not only did the black elite seek to uplift the subaltern classes, it also recog-nized the imperative need for racial solidarity" (*"Doers of the Word": African-American Women Speakers and Writers in the North (1830–1880)* [New York: Oxford University Press, 1995], 12).

25. See Sterling Stuckey, *Slave Culture: Nationalist Theory and the Foundations of Black America* (New York: Oxford University Press, 1987), 196. Stuckey's contention that all black Americans are basically African in culture is not directly borne out in Dorr's text but indirectly in Dorr's race pride and conscious affiliations with African cultures (vii). Houston Baker in *The Journey Back: Issues in Black Literature and Criticism* (Chicago: University of Chicago Press, 1980) argues that black

writers' identities are contradictorily constructed because the very entry into language signals a distance from the slave community (xvii). Henry Louis Gates in *The Signifying Monkey* shows that trickster figures create ambivalence and double voicing in African-American writing.

26. Mary-Suzanne Schriber, "Julia Ward Howe and the Travel Book," *New England Quarterly* 62 (1989): 267, 269.

27. See William W. Stowe, *Going Abroad: European Travel in Nineteenth-Century American Culture* (Princeton: Princeton University Press, 1994), 13, and Christopher Mulvey, *Transatlantic Manners: Social Patterns in Nineteenth-Century Anglo-American Travel Literature* (Cambridge: Cambridge University Press, 1990), 7.

28. Pierre Bourdieu, *Distinction*, 53–54.

29. Bourdieu, *Distinction,* 3.

30. Frederick Douglass, *My Bondage and My Freedom* (New York: Arno, 1968), 365–66.

31. Mulvey, *Transatlantic Manners,* 7.

32. Thus, although the enormously popular Nathaniel Parker Willis began his *Pencillings By the Way* with an account of the cholera in Paris, he went on to present his travels as cultural acquisition: "I have devoted a week to the museum at Naples. It is a world! Any thing like a full description of it would tire even an antiquary. It is one of those things (and there are many in Europe) that fortunately *compel* travel" (*Pencillings By the Way*, 2 vols. [Philadelphia: Carey, Lea and Blanchard, 1836], 1:75).

33. Sandra Tomc, "An Idle Industry: Nathaniel Parker Willis and the Workings of Literary Leisure," *American Quarterly* 49 (December 1997): 783.

34. Bayard Taylor, *Views A-Foot; Or Europe Seen with Knapsack and Staff* (Philadelphia: David McKay, 1890), 10, 59.

35. Taylor, *Views A-Foot,* 72.

36. See Malini Johar Schueller, *U.S. Orientalisms: Race, Nation, and Gender in Literature, 1790–1890* (Ann Arbor: University of Michigan Press, 1998), 1–3.

37. George William Curtis, *The Howadji in Syria* (New York: Hurst and Company, 1852), 9.

38. Curtis, *The Howadji in Syria,* 17.

39. Stowe, *Going Abroad,* 12.

40. Stowe, *Going Abroad,* 71.

41. William Wells Brown, "The American Fugitive in Europe: Sketches of Places and People Abroad," in *The Travels of William Wells Brown*, ed. Paul Jefferson (New York: Markus Wiener, 1991), 98.

42. Frederick Douglass, *Life and Times of Frederick Douglass* (New York: Bonanza Books), 244.

43. Nancy Prince, *A Black Woman's Odyssey through Russia and Jamaica: The Narrative of Nancy Prince* (New York: Markus Wiener, 1990), 54.

44. Griffiths's "Letters" were serialized in *Douglass' Monthly*. See especially the April 1859 issue, 54–55.

45. Cheryl Fish points out Nancy Prince's attraction to the "colonizing paradigm with its assumption of Western superiority and endorsement of empire" ("Voices of Restless (Dis)continuity: The Significance of Travel for Free Black Women in the Antebellum Americas," *Women's Studies* 26 [1997]: 479).

46. Prince, *Black Woman's Odyssey*, 54.

47. A good example of an African-American travel narrative that offers accounts of "native" customs and lifestyles through a privileged observer, but is clearly written as a corrective to Anglo accounts of African countries, is Robert Campbell's *A Pilgrimage to My Motherland: An Account of a Journey Among the Egbas and Yorubas of Central Africa in 1859–60* (New York: Thomas Hamilton, 1861).

48. Dennis Harris, *A Summer on the Borders of the Caribbean Sea* (New York: Negro Universities Press, 1969).

49. Henry Louis Gates, introduction to *Our Nig; or, Sketches from the Life of a Free Black* (New York: Random House, 1983).

50. Fuad Sha'ban, *Islam and Arabs in Early American Thought: The Roots of Orientalism in America* (Durham, N.C.: Acorn Press, 1991). Subsequently, William W. Stowe discussed *A Colored Man* in *Going Abroad,* 61–67, 133–34. See also Malini Johar Schueller's *U.S. Orientalisms* for a discussion of *A Colored Man* in relation to Near East travel writing, 105–8.

51. The idea of identity as performance has been suggested by Judith Butler in *Gender Trouble: Feminism and the Subversion of Identity* (New York: Routledge, 1990). Butler, however, thinks only in terms of gender and not race.

52. See Matthew J. Brucolli, ed., *The Profession of Authorship in America, 1800–1870: The Papers of William Charvat* (Columbus: Ohio State University Press, 1968), 292–93.

53. See Henry Highland Garnet, *The Past and Present Condition, and the Destiny of the Colored Races* (Miami, Fla.: Mnemosyne, 1969), 6–7, 12.

54. Stowe, *Going Abroad,* 62.

55. James Clifford, "Traveling Cultures," in *Cultural Studies,* ed. Lawrence Grossberg, Cary Nelson, and Paula Treichler (New York: Routledge, 1992), 106. Mary Prince's *The History of Mary Prince* is a good example of the very different kind of "travel" experienced by slaves as compared to Anglo-Americans.

56. Minstrel shows were advertised with great frequency all through the late 1850s and early 1860s. The *Cleveland Daily Review* announced, "We see by the bills that the Morris Bros., Pell and Trowbridge Troupe of Ethiopian singers, imitators, and caricaturists, are to hold forth to-night at the Melodeon" (September 11, 1858). The *Cleveland Daily Plain Dealer* advertised Hooley & Campbell thus: "Wherever this company go they meet with brilliant success, and beyond a doubt they are the best band now before the public" (June 2, 1860, 3).

57. *Daily Cleveland Herald,* September 17, 1858, 4.

58. *Cleveland Plain Dealer,* September 20, 1858, 3.

59. I want to thank Bradley Dilger for pointing this out to me.

60. See Edward Said, *Orientalism* (New York: Pantheon, 1978), 138.

61. Douglass's commencement address to the Western Reserve College, "The Claims of the Negro Ethnologically Considered," received laudatory notice in the *Cleveland Plain Dealer* (July 14, 1854). The notice makes no mention of Dorr, however.

A COLORED MAN ROUND THE WORLD

A COLORED MAN

ROUND THE WORLD.

———————

BY A QUADROON.

———————

PRINTED FOR THE AUTHOR.
1858.

TO MY SLAVE MOTHER.

MOTHER! wherever thou art, whether in Heaven or a lesser world; or whether around the freedom Base of a Bunker Hill, or only at the lowest savannah of American Slavery, thou art the same to me, and I dedicate this token of my knowledge to thee mother, Oh, my own mother!

YOUR DAVID.

Bunker Hill: Early battle of the American Revolution, fought on June 17, 1775, which validated the moral victory of the Americans.

INDEX.

PREFACE.

THE Author of this book, though a quadroon, is pleased to announce himself the "Colored man around the world." Not because he may look at a colored man's position as an honorable one at this age of the world, he is too smart for that, but because he has the satisfaction of looking with his own eyes and reason at the ruins of the ancestors of which he is the posterity. If the ruins of the Author's ancestors were not a living language of their scientific majesty, this book could receive no such appellation with pride. Luxor, Carnack, the Memnonian and the Pyramids make us exclaim, "What monuments of pride can surpass these? what genius must have reflected on their foundations! what an ambition these people must have given to the rest of the world when found the "glory of the world in their hieroglyphic stronghold of learning," whose stronghold, to-day, is not to be battered down, because we cannot reach their hidden alphabet. Who is as one, we might suppose, "learned in all the learning of the Egyptians." Have we as learned a man as Moses, and if yes, who can prove it? How did he come to do what no man can do now? You answer, God aided him; that is not the question! No, all you know about it is he was "learned in all the learning of the Egyptians," that is the answer; and thereby knew how to facilitate a glorious cause at heart, because had he been less learned, who could conceive how he could have proved to us to be a man full of successful logic. Well, who were the Egyptians? Ask Homer if their lips were not thick, their hair curly, their feet flat and their skin black.

But the Author of this book, though a colored man, hopes to die believing that this federated government is destined to be the noblest fabric ever germinated in the brain of men or the tides of Time. Though a colored man, he believes that he has the right

---

Quadroon: A person with one-quarter black ancestry.

to say that, in his opinion, *the American people are to be the Medes and Persians of the 19th century.* He believes, from what he has seen in the four quarters of the globe, that the federal tribunal of this mighty people and territory, are to weigh other nations' portion of power by its own scale, and equipoise them on its own pivot, "*the will of the whole people,*" the federal people. And as he believes that the rights of ignorant people, whether white or black, ought to be respected by those who have seen more, he offers this book of travels to that class who craves to know what those know who have respect for them. In offering this book to the public, I will say, by the way, I wrote it under the disadvantage of having access to no library save Walker's school dictionary. In traveling through Europe, Asia and Africa, I am indebted to Mr. Cornelius Fellowes, of the highly respectable firm of Messrs. Fellowes & Co., 149 Common St., New Orleans, La. This gentleman treated me as his own son, and could look on me as as free a man as walks the earth. But if local law has power over man, instead of man's effects, I was legally a slave, and would be to-day, like my mother, were I on Louisiana's soil instead of Ohio's

When we returned to America, after a three years' tour, I called on this original man to consummate a two-fold promise he made me, in different parts of the world, because I wanted to make a connection, that I considered myself more than equaled in dignity and means, but as he refused me on old bachelor principles, I fled from him and his princely promises, westward, where the "star of empire takes its way," reflecting on the moral liberties of the legal freedom of England, France and our New England States, with the determination to write this book of "overlooked things" in the four quarters of the globe, seen by "a colored man round the world."

THE AUTHOR.

"star of empire takes its way": An echo of Irish-born idealist philosopher George Berkeley (1685–1753). Berkeley's famous line "Westward the course of Empire takes its way" was quoted by many politicians and writers of the nineteenth century, including John Adams and Ralph Waldo Emerson.

DEBUT IN A FOREIGN LAND.

This day, June 15th, 1851, I commence my writings of a promiscuous voyage. This day is Sunday. I am going from the Custom house, where I have deposited my baggage to be searched for contraband goods, and making my way along a street that might be termed, from its appearance, "The street of cemeteries." This street is in Liverpool, and is a mercantile street in every sense of the word, and the reason why it looked so lonesome and a business street at that, is wanting. I must now explain why so great a street looked dismal. The English people are, indeed, a moral people. This was the Sabbath, and the "bells were chiming," discoursing the sweetest sacred music I had ever heard. The streets were very narrow and good. Their material was solid square stones closely packed together. The houses were very high, some being six stories. Not one house for half a mile had a door or window ajar. It was raining; consequently not a person was to be seen. All of a sudden the coachman drew up to the side walk, and, opening the coach, said, "Adelphi, sir." I was looking

with considerable interest to see the hotel of so much celebrity on board the ship. Captain Riley had informed me
that it was a house not to be surpassed in the "hotel line,"
and I had put an estimated interest on this important item
to travelers that Southerners are too much addicted to. I
mean to say, that I, a Southerner, judge too much by
appearance, instead of experience. I had been taught at
Orleans that the "English could whip all the world, and we
could whip the English," and that England was always in
great danger of being starved by us, and all her manufactories stopped in double quick time by Southern cotton-
planters. But, the greatest absurdity of all was, that England was very much afraid that we would declare war against
her, and thereby ruin what little independence she still
retains. I, under this dispensation of knowledge, looked
around to see the towering of a "St. Charles or Verandah,"
but when I saw a house looking like all the rest, I came to
the conclusion that the English were trying to get along
without making any improvement, as it was not certain how
long we would permit her to remain a "monarchial independent nation." Just then a well-dressed gentleman
opened the door and descended the steps with an umbrella
to escort me in. "Come right in here, sir," said he, leading me into a large room, with an organ and hat-stands as
its furniture. The organ was as large as an ordinary sized
church organ. The gentleman took my overcoat and hung
it up. He then asked me some questions concerning the

voyage, after which he asked me to walk to the Bureau and register my name. This done we ascend one flight of stairs and enter my room. He asked me if I wished fire. I answered in the affirmative. He left me.

Having seated myself *a la American*, I listened very attentively to "those chiming bells." Tap, tap on my door called forth another American expression, "come in." The door opened and a beautiful girl of fifteen summers came in with a scuttle of coal and kindling. She wore on her head a small frilled cap, and it was very small. A snow white apron adorned her short, neat dress. A man is a good deal like a dog in some particulars. He may be uncommonly savage in his nature, and as soon as he sees his sexual mate, his attention is manifested in the twinkling of an eye. She looked so neat, I thought it good policy to be polite, and become acquainted. Having finished making a lively little fire, she rose up from her half-bending posture to follow up her duty through the hotel. "What is your name, Miss," said I; "Mary," said she, at the same time moving away. "I shall be here a week said I, and want you to take care of me." Mary's pretty little feet could stay no longer with propriety the first time.

In fifteen minutes the gong rang for dinner. I locked my door, and made my way through the narrow passages to hunt head quarters. Passing one of the inferior passage ways, I saw Mary half whispering to one of her companions about the American, and laughing jocularly. Her eyes fell upon me just as mine did on her. In the twinkling of an eye she conveyed an idea to her comrade that the topic must be something else, which seemed to have been understood before conveyed. "Mary," said I, "I want some washing done," as polite as a piled basket of chips. She stepped up to me and said, "Are they ready, sir?" "No, said I, "I will be up in a few minutes, (we always do things by minutes.) "I will call for them," said she. I descended and found a good dinner, after which I walked into the news-room, where I found several of the merchants of Liverpool assembled to read and discuss the prevailing topics of interest. Seated close to a table on which was the London Times, New York Tribune and Herald, the French Journal, called the Moniteur, besides several other Journals of lesser note, was a noble looking gentleman. On the other side of this feast of news was another noble and intellectual looking gentleman. These were noblemen from different parts of England. They were quietly discussing the weak points in American policy. One held that if the negroes of the Southern States were fit for freedom, it would be an easy matter for four million of slaves to raise the standard of liberty, and maintain it against 250,000 slaveholders. The other gentleman held that it was very true, but they needed some white man, well posted in the South, with courage enough to plot the *entree.* He continued, at great length, to show the feasibility under a French plotter. He closed with this expression, " One intelligent Frenchman like Ledru

---

Ledru Rollin: Alexandre Auguste Ledru-Rollin (1807–1874), French politician.

Rollin could do the whole thing before it could be known."
I came to the conclusion that they were not so careful in the
expression of their views as I thought they ought to be. I
was quite sure that they would not be allowed to use such
treasonable language at Orleans or Charleston as that they
had just indulged in.

Sitting in my room about an hour after hearing this nau-
seous language, Mary came for the clothes, for that is what
she asked for. I requested Mary to wait until Monday
morning, for the fact was, I had no clothes — they were in
the Custom House. Here Mary began to show more familiarity than I had ever shown, but she only expressed
enough to show me that she only wished to return for my
clothes when they were ready. I gave her to understand
that nothing would give me more pleasure than to have her
return again for them.

Two weeks have gone by. I am now packing my trunk
for London. In half an hour, the evening express train
leaves here for a five hours' cruise over farms of rich and
poor, like a streak of lightning. I find on the day of departure that the servants are like the servants of all parts
of my own country. It is impossible for me to do anything
for myself. I have offers from nearly all parts of the Hotel,
volunteering to do all that is to be done and more too.—
Before I commenced packing my trunk, I went down to the

Bureau (office) to have my bill made out. As I passed
along the passage I saw a large man with slippers on, with
a cap denoting Cookery, bowing and scraping. I instantly
perceived that my fame, as an American, had reached the
culinary sanctum. I requested the Clerk to have my bill
ready, but found that I was too late in the information to
be given. My bill was already made out.

A quarter to 5 o'clock, I showed to Mary, my sincere
wishes for her welfare, and left my apartment. Her cap
was neater than when I located there; her apron was
whiter, and her hair was neater. I done my duty to the
advice given by Murray, who is the author of the Guide
Book of all Europe, Asia, and even Africa. He says that it
is best to give a small bonus to the menials in public or
private houses. The landlord, saw me in the coach and
wished me a happy voyage to London. When the coach
moved gradually away from that small Hotel, it carried
lingering thoughts of friendship and comfort. I thought of
the kind attention, and obedient but commanding language
of all I had seen, and the moral came home to my heart,
saying "you have value received." I reflected on Mary's
cap and snow white apron; the old porter's hopeful countenance; the dining room servants; and how well they
seemed to be pleased, when the driver stopped my coach and
landed me at the London station in a good humor. All
aboard! The Cars, (express train in a hurry) dashed on

with fury, and I found myself a happy man on my way to London.

LONDON.

LAST NIGHT I arrived here, making the time from Liverpool in five hours and a half. My location is between Buckingham Palace and Trafalgar Square. I am on the second floor, in the Trafalgar Hotel, on Trafalgar Square. The Queen, when in London, resides at this celebrated palace. It is in St. James' Park. This July 28th, London is the world's Bazaar. The Crystal Palace is the acquafortis of curiosity that gives the arcadial polish to London's greatness. This is the place where every country is trying to make a pigmy of some other. In this great feast of genius no country is fairly represented. The United States has many articles of arts in the palace that are not what she has ever prided herself on as her arts. One of our ordinary Steam Boats would have astonished the natives beyond the admiration of all the trumpery that we ever contemplate carrying to a World's Fair. I was, indeed, ashamed to see the piles of India Rubber Shoes, Coats and Pants, and Clocks that stood out in bas relief in that part of the

---

The Queen: Queen Victoria. She ascended to the throne in 1837 and was the queen until her death in 1901.
Crystal Palace: Built in London in 1850 by Joseph Paxton for the Great Exhibition of 1851, which drew over six million visitors from all over the world and displayed close to one million items. The structure, made almost entirely of glass, was unique in its time. It became an important symbol of the primacy of the British Empire. Dorr is as awestruck as any tourist, but focuses, interestingly, on the vulgar race among nations

palace appropriated to the American Arts and Sciences.—
Pegged Shoes and Boots were without number. Martingales
and Side Saddles, Horse Shoes, Ploughs, Threshing Machines, Irrigators, and all the most worthless trash to be
found in the States. I saw everything that was a prevailing
disgrace to our country except slaves. I understood that a
South Carolinian proposed taking half a dozen haughty
and sinewy negroes to the Fair, but was only deterred from
that proposition by the want of courage to risk six fat, strong
healthy negroes to the chances of escape from slavery to
freedom. In the centre of this beautiful and most splendid
palace, was a Band of Music not to be surpassed by any
Band for discoursing sweet melody. Close to this music
was a beautiful fountain, throwing sprays upward like
the heaves of a shark; and round about this fountain were
seats for ladies and gentlemen to take refreshments together. This palace resembles, in a great degree, "Paradise
found;" there is also some sparrows inside yet, that the
Falcons did not run out when those twenty thousand took
possession some months ago. These little birds light about
among this gay crowd as if they were on one of our wild
prairies, lighting among the still gayer tribe of flora. Two
or three tried to light on a spray of water, but could not
make it go. I see two sitting on a piano, whilst one is trying
to get an equilibrium on the strings of a harp. The piano
now opens and a noblemen is seating one of the most
handsome women there I have seen in England. I said

---

to make "pigmies" of each other. As a proud American, he ridicules
the trash displayed in the U.S. section, but also takes the opportunity,
by bringing slavery to the fore, to impugn the very desirability of being
American.

to a young Englishman, that is indeed a handsome woman. He said yes, she is generally pronounced the handsomest woman in London. I enquired her pedigree and found that it was the benevolent Duchess of Sutherland; like a humming bird, from one "sweet flower" to another her alabaster-like fingers darted from the bassiest note to the flutiest. The pianos were generally enclosed like a separate tomb with railings a yard from the pianos. After her highness had played out "God Save the Queen" and brought an audience round the railing, as if they really came to protect the "queen of beauty," she played a thrilling retreat as if her intention was to convey the idea that she must retreat or be captured. The piece played, she rose straight up and gazed around upon the recruits she had drummed up with the air of a successful adventurer throughout the world; she moved along this immense crowd of various classes like a swan in a showery storm. Whilst all was in commotion, she seemed more herself. The noble gallant seemed to be quite conscious that the lady he was gallanting was the *Duchess of Sutherland.*

On the outside of the Crystal Palace is a small, fairy-like house, erected for Prince Albert and her majesty the Queen of England to lunch in when they visit the Fair. It is said that the Prince planned it himself. In this pretty little house is enough furniture of various beauties to make an ordinary Fair itself.

The Police regulations about this Fair are admirable.

Prince Albert: Married Queen Victoria in 1840.

There is no question that can be asked about this affair but will be properly and intellectually answered by any policeman. They are intelligent men and seem to take an interest as well as pride in this great Fair.

————

THE QUEEN IN HYDE PARK.

IT is now 4 o'clock. All the streets within a mile of the Crystal Palace are crowded with people, instead of drays, carts, wagons and other impeding obstacles to the World's Fair. For a quarter of a mile down the street that leads to St. James' Square, where the Queen resides, at Buckingham Palace, I presume I can see 50,000 people bareheaded, that is to say, they have their hats off. But, at the further end of this quarter of a mile, I see a uniform commotion, and this commotion of heads are coming towards Hyde Park. I mean only the commotion but not the heads. These heads are being responded to from an open plain Calashe, that is coming as rapid as a Post Chaise from the battle field when bringing good tidings to a King.— The object of this exciting moment is the Queen of England. One minute and she is gone by, as she passed me, bowing on all sides to the crowd greeting her. I felt a sort of religious thrill pass over me, and I said to myself "this is civilization."

Her Majesty was evidently proud of her people's homage; and her people were not ashamed to show their loyalty to their "gracious Queen." She was looking remarkably healthy for one living on the delicacies of a Queen. In fact she was too healthy in appearance for a Queen. Her color was too red and masculine for a lady. She was considerable stouter than I thought she was, and quite as handsome as I expected to find the great Queen. Seated opposite her, face to face, was her Maid of Honor; and seated by her side vis-a-vis to the Queen, was a couple of the "little bloods" of her Majesty and Prince Coburgh. I thought it strange that his highness, Prince Albert, was not accompanying the Queen. I learned afterwards that it was usual for the Queen to go in Hyde Park alone. I also found that the Prince and his courtiers were gone out deer stalking.

In the Queen's calashe was four greys. The driver rode the hindmost left horse. In his right hand he carried a light whip which was altogether useless. About 50 yards ahead of this moving importance, a liveried outrider sped on at a rapid speed, that the populace might know that he was soliciting their attention to making way for the Queen. He wore long, white-legged boots, and held his Arab steed as artful as a Bedouin sporting over a rocky desert. His other habiliments were red, save his hat, which was a latest style silk. The driver keeps him in view, and has nothing to do but mount and drive off after this courier or out-rider, who gets his orders at the Palace where to lead.

It is said that the Queen is not celebrated for a good temper. Like her symbol, the lion, she is not to be bearded by any one, no matter how important. She is a natural monarch and feels her royalty. Prince Albert is one of the handsomest men I ever saw. The like of the Prince's popularity among the ladies of the Court cannot be equaled by any nobleman in England; but that popularity must be general, it cannot be in spots, for the Queen is not unlike other women under the influence of the "green-eyed monster. Although Prince Albert's virtue has never been dishonored by even a hint, still the Queen is not to be too trusty. Prince Albert is a model of a "true gentleman." He could not suspect half as quick as the most virtuous Queen the world has ever been ornamented with.

The English people are alone in all things pertaining to domestic life. It would puzzle the double-width intellect of a hermit to tell what oné was thinking about; and this nonchalence of air to surrounding circumstances is every moment blowing upon the object in their heart. France sets the fashion for the world, but what the morning paper say about the dress worn by the empress on the champs d'elysee yesterday, is not what the poorest maid servant is trying to find out to cut her calico by, but what her Majesty wore at Windsor or Buckingham. These people were wearing the skins of the beasts of their forests in the days of the Cæsars' invasion, and barbarous as our Indians, but now they are the most civilized and christian power on this earth.

"green-eyed monster": Jealousy, in Shakespeare's *Othello.*

A German now sitting by my side tells me this is a gross subject for me to be writing upon. I asked what subject? He said Konigon (Queen). On reflection I find it true, and now retire from the heading of this chapter.

I AM GOING TO PARIS.

I AM now all cap a pie for Paris. Ho! for Boston, is nothing to ah! Paris. I have been this morning to get my last view of the great Palace of the World's Fair. I have since been to Greenwich to eat white bait, and I am now hurrying on to the station. Whoever wishes to see a good deal of the country, and a broken down route, had better take what is called the Brighton Route. If you leave London at 6 o'clock in the evening, you will stop at 8 o'clock at New Haven, a place with a name on the map, but in fact no place at all, save the destination of the train of this route. There you will, in all probability, have to wait about an old building an hour or two for the arrival of a boat to take you across the channel. Next morning, if you are lucky, you arrive at 8 o'clock at a little old French town called Dieppe, just in time to be too late to take the morning train for Paris. It is said that these little old half dead towns live off these tricks. I got a pretty breakfast *a la carte;* I say pretty, because I had boiled eggs, red wine and white, radishes, lettuce, and three boquets on my breakfast table. Having been disappointed in taking the morning's train for Paris, I vented my wrath on both bottles of wine, thereby getting an equilibrium between disappointment and contentment. This done I went down to a little old shed which they called the Custom House, to get my trunks which they had been searching. I then took a ride in the country to see the ruins of an ancient castle, captured by the first reigning king of the present great Bourbon family, Henry Quatre, King of Navarre. This was the first ruined castle I had ever seen, and it interested me so much that in spite of the boat last night with no berths, sea sickness, custom-house troubles, disappointment in getting to Paris that day instead of 11 o'clock at night, I was in quite a good humor, and in fact, considered myself well paid for the ride, though in an old chaise and two poor horses.

At the ruins of this enormous pile of brick and mortar, was an old, broken down French officer. His companion was a lonely raven. We could go in and out of no part of this dilapidated mass of downfallen power, without meeting the raven. He seemed to be a lonely spirit. I caught at him once when he came within two feet of me; he jumped about a foot further off and stopped right still, and turned his head so that one eye was up and the other down, and kept looking up at me as long as I looked at him, as if he would fain say *laissi moi* (let me be). The cool treatment of the raven about these old ruins lowered my spirits. I gave the old soldier a franc for his trouble and information, and got in my old turn-out, and turned around to say adieu to the old soldier when I found him too much engaged paying Jocko with crumbs, his portion of the bonus, for services rendered.

At 4 o'clock I found myself well seated in a French car, for the first time, direct for Paris. Here we go in a tunnel, and it is dark as ebony; here we come out; away go the cattle as if Indians were after them.

It would be impossible to conjecture that French farmers were lazy, for this is the Sabbath and down in the meadows I see farmers reaping. I can see towns in such quick succession, it would be useless to attempt to describe them. It is now 11 o'clock, and I am at my destination and being searched. Nothing found and I am pronounced an honest man. But my honesty, if there be any, is like Falstaff's, hid. I have two hundred cigars in my over and under coat, and they are, indeed, contraband and was one of the greatest objects of search; but, reader, if you pronounce this French stupidity you deceive yourself. It was French politeness that allowed me to pass unnoticed by this scrutinizing assemblage of Savans. If a man move among these lynx-eyed prefectures as a gentleman ought to, he is, once out of three times, likely to pass the barrier of their polite inclinations, whilst at the same time it would give them great

---

Falstaff: Good-humored, egotistical character in Shakespeare's *Henry IV, Part 1, Henry IV, Part 2,* and *The Merry Wives of Windsor.* The numerous literary references in Dorr's book should caution us against taking Dorr at his own word in the preface where he suggests that he had very little learning and no access to books.

satisfaction to believe that it would pay to examine you, were there a justifiable excuse for such rudeness, overbalancing the politeness which is characteristic of their whole national dignity.   The French are proud of their national characteristics, and least of all nations inclined to trample them under foot.

It is now eleven o'clock, as I have before said, and I am in Paris, trying to get across the Boulevard des Italian. What I mean by trying is, picking my chance.   I am no dancing master, and in this crowded street might not do the dodging right the first time.

I am now across and ringing the bell at 179 Rue Richelieu.   This is the Hotel des Prince (Hotel of the Princes). Mr. Privat is the proprietor.   In this Hotel all have gone to bed except a beautiful little woman at the concierge.   She was sewing whilst stillness reigned around her, like a deep, dark forest, just before a storm.   She received me with a smile.   I, not knowing that this was her usual behavior to all patronage of this or any other house in Paris, took for granted I had made an extra impression right off.   She took me to an apartment which she said was merely temporary. To-morrow, she said, I could get another to my taste.   I gazed around at all the different doors and comforts with numerous conveniencies of neatness, and said to her, "Miss, this, in my opinion, is good enough for the oldest inhabitant." She smiled and went away and brought me a bottle of water with a piece of ice inside just the shape of the bottle.   "How did you put that piece of ice inside without breaking the bottle?" said I. "It was water, sir, and it froze inside," said she, "will you have something to eat?" I said I would like a small bit of chicken and red wine; she rang the bell and an English and French waiter was summoned; she went away and left me pretty certain that I was in Paris.

———

FIRST DAY IN PARIS.

NEXT morning I felt pretty sure I was in Paris, or I "wasn't anywhere else." Every five minutes would assure me that I was there. Before the grey of the morn departed from Paris I had two lady visitors. One was a beautiful girl, like "Mary of Adelphi." She was evidently mistaken in finding a tenant in this one of her rooms, unless that was her way. She moved up to the washstand, which was near my bed, or rather couch, and slyly looked in the drawer and drew back. I, wishing to let her know that if her business or adventure was connected with me, she need not fear waking me, rose my left arm and said, "good morning!" She, not understanding what I did say, muttered out something like "*reste vous tranquilles*," which, I afterwards learned, meant, don't be disturbed. She hurried out the half opened door pulling her little starched dress, that seemed to pull back, after her. Five minutes after this, she returned and placed on my stand close to my bed, a bottle of ice water and a glass. I asked her name, she said, Elverata, and winded away.

Five minutes after this another female opened my door about a foot and leaned gracefully in. She asked me some question two or three times, all that I could understand was Blanche, with some other points to it like *E sirs*. Consulting my guide of the French translated into the four following languages, French, Italian, German and English, I discovered she was talking about washing. I got this book in London and studied all the way to Paris, but found that I had made no improvement; all I knew of the book was, that the words translated were only some useful words that the solicitors would most likely know themselves when it would be necessary to use such expressions. She ran to me, for she was acquainted with the book better than I was, and helped to find what she wished to say. "*Ie trouver, Ie trouver*," she said. I gave her the book, at the same time asking her in English what was *trouver*. She looked up at the wall, like a Madonna, and seemed to be lost in inward study, at last she looked me full in the face and said, "fyend." "Ah!" said I, "find." "Yis!" said she, "what you call *cela?*" "Washerwoman," said I. *Ie suis washe-women.*" This woman was certainly very bewitching whilst speaking this broken English. I gave her to understand

---

"Ie trouver, Ie trouver": "I find, I find." The substitution of *I* for *J* was common up to the nineteenth century.

that some other time would be more agreeable. She said she "stand" and went out; but as she did not stand, but went out, I presume she meant to say "I understand."

At eight o'clock I descended to the *salle a manger* for breakfast. Persons were coming in to breakfast, two and three a minute, and others were going out as fast. This continued till eleven o'clock. Thirty and forty were frequently at the table at the same time. Mostly all were Europeans; and had everything not gone on so regularly, an American "greenhorn" would have taken them to be the confusion of tongues convening for a reconciliation. On the table was more wine than coffee. The coffee was usually taken in the smoking room, where all gentlemen assemble to discuss politics. Among this assemblage that I am so flippantly speaking of, was three noblemen of England, one Duke of Italy, three barons of the Rhine, and a broken down princess. From merely gossip authority, I learned that she was the wife of a great man in one of the Russio Turko principalities. She was generally dressed in black, and had two servants and a *lacquey de place*. She was handsome and that had ruined her. She was getting from her husband 100,000 per annum to stay away from him and his court, which seemed to meet her approbation. She roomed on the same floor I did, and I frequently met her smiling in these narrow and dark passage ways. She seldom dined at the *"table de hote,"* (dinner table) but either at the

---

salle a manger: Dining room.
lacquey de place: Footman.

trois frere, (three brothers) or the *maison d'or Doree,* corner of the Boulevard and rue Lafitte. She most always had her Cabinet, good dinners and various wines, consequently was always full of agreeability. She would walk home herself, and, like the rest of ladies in Paris, she was always sure that her dress in front should not drag the ground, by a process she had in her nature, to show her intention of keeping her dress high enough to prevent all accidents of the kind. By this habit of hers, she got many admirers, for what a man would then see instead of her dress would be no disadvantage to her or her intention. Her reputation was such that had she been once gazed upon by the Virgin Mary, the fiery censure of her pure eyes would have been basilisks to her poor heart; the poor Princess would have dropped dead from the mere spark of censure which the Virgin could not, though fain would, hold back.

The day has gone by. I stood about, looking! looking! looking! Seeing what is novel enough to an American in Paris, in the court of the *Hotel des Princes.* Night came on and I went to my room to prepare to see a "Night in Paris." I shall write of a Night in Paris, and then shall say no more of Paris until I have been to Germany and return, where I expect to spend three or four months. After this voyage I calculate to spend the winter here, and write something of Paris and its manners.

My first day ends by meeting the Princess on the steps, and having the pleasure of answering some inquiries of

---

maison d'or Doree: Gilded House.

hers about sea-sickness, and pleasant ships of the Cunard Line.

———

FIRST NIGHT IN PARIS.

My "first day in Paris" commenced at night. If sauce for the goose is sauce for the gander, I will commence this chapter in the day by saying, "where now! valet de place?" "Notre dame," he replied, and the coachman drove away towards the Boulevards. In half an hour's time, he reined before the door of that "Venerable old monument of reality and romance." I approached it like a timid child being baited with a shining sixpence. As my feet touched the sill, a peal came from the belfry, one of those sonorous twangs, that have made so many hearts flinch for hundreds of years in the "Bloody Bastile," and it vibrated from my timid heart to all parts of my frame. At this moment a reverend father offered me his hand, who had all the time been concealed beneath what one might well take to be a dark black coffin standing on end. I accepted his hand, and he led me quietly in that vast "sepulchre of kings."

In all directions I saw magnificent aisles, and altars

"Notre dame": Famous cathedral in Paris, built in the twelfth century.

with burning incense. Magnificent pictures representing all reverend worth, from the "Son of Man," to saints of France. Golden knobs with inscriptions thereon, adorned the footsteps of every visitor thereof, denoting the downwardness of kings who had once ruled nations. Whilst standing there awestruck with departed worth, I gazed downward with a submissive heart, when lo! I stood upon the coffin of a king! I quickly changed my position, but stepped upon a queen. The valet was relating to me the many different opinions the people had about stepping on noted personages, and how unnecessary it was to take notice of such things as they were dead, when I got disgusted at his ignorance, and stepped from a Queen to a Princess.

To describe this gorgeously furnished sanctum, it is enough to say, that all the brilliant artists of this scientific people have been engaged for hundreds of years in its decoration. Not only employed by the coffers of the Church of France, but by the throne that upheld numerous kings, as well as the wish of the whole populace of France, and the spoils of other nations. Hundreds of people from different parts of the world visit it every day, and all leave a franc or two. Thousands of Parisians visit it every day, and they make no mark of decay. It stands a living monument of Church and State.

Drive me to the national assembly, I said to the coachman. In ten minutes I was going up the gallery. Before

I went in, the valet went to a member's coachman, and gave him a franc, and he gave in return a ticket to the gallery. Each member is allowed so many gallery tickets, and if he fails in giving them out, he makes his servants presents of them, and they sell them.

They were debating republican principles. Louis Napoleon was then President of the Republic, and on the door of every building and gate of France were these words in legible letters, "Liberte Eqalite Fraternite." Louis Napoleon was not there that day, and they seemed to have a good time, like mice when the cat is away. The most incomprehensible part of their proceeding was, sometimes two would be speaking at once, regardless of the chair. The speaker hammered away furiously, but it was hard to tell, unless you knew, whether he was beating up a revival or a retreat from destruction; as they cooled off their debative heat, there was always twenty or thirty ready to throw agitating fuel in the furnace. As they would cool down a whiff, mushroom-like risings, would be perceptible in four or five different parts of the spacious hall. I could make nothing out of what was going on, save willingness to talk instead of listening, and I left. One handsome and intelligent looking gentleman descended at the same time, which I learned to be the correspondent of the New York Tribune. I then took a curve like tour back, across the Seine, by the Tuillieries, Luxomburg, and back to the same part of the Boulevards, which was more crowded with

Louis Napoleon: Dorr's travels occurred during a tumultuous period in French history when workers rioted and vacillated between republicanism and monarchy. According to his records, Dorr was in France between June and December 1851. Louis Napoleon, who had been imprisoned by royalist forces, escaped and was elected president of the French Republic in December 1848. In 1851, he engineered a coup d'état and forced a plebiscite in favor of a new constitution that gave the president monarchical powers. Louis Napoleon proclaimed himself Emperor Napoleon III in 1852.

fashion, than when I passed along in the forenoon, and went home. Night came on, and with it, the gayest time of Paris. The valet said I must go to *Jardin mabeille*, (a ball), I rode there. This is a nightly ball, but there was no less than fifty vehicles of different comforts, which showed that a great many foreigners were there, because Parisians generally prefer promenading when going to such a feast of pleasure. I paid two francs and went in.

It was a garden about a square block in size. In all parts of it was shrubbery of the most fragrant odors. There was an immense number of little walks, with neat rustic seats for lovers to caress in, from the disinterested eye; and on my first preambulation, I got lost, and intruded more than was polite, but I did not know the importance of this discretion, until I perilously saw the danger. Had I gone on without stopping, I would have led myself to the orchestra, where and when I could have taken part in the amusement to the approbation of all present. When I discovered that I did not know what I was about, I stopped quickly and looked scrutinizingly around those snug little bowers. All in a minute out came a "bower lover," as furious as a cat. I asked him "where the ball was;" he discovered that I was no Frenchman, and could not have meant intrusion; he directed me to go straight ahead, and I left him in his bliss.

Like a round pigeon house on the end of pole, I pronounce the orchestra. A stair ran up to the pigeon house from the platform round the great pole, or post that supported it. A small enclosure was under the orchestra and occasionally the band would descend to the platform to play. Round this orchestra they danced. The spectators seemed to be exclusively foreigners; they made a ring around the gay lotharios as unbroken as the one they made around the orchestra. The bassy and fluty melodious Band, discoursed the sweetest waltz that ever tickled my admiration. Off they glided like a scared serpent, winding their curvy way as natural as if they were taking their chances. There they come! But there is some still going in the ranks, and there is still a vacancy. Twice they have made the circuit, and the hoop is complete. Now to me it is all dizziness, and it all looked to me as a moving body of muses from times of yore. Occasionally my eye would cling to a couple for an instant, but this was occasioned by the contrast between a large, fat, and heavy gentleman, that had become a troublesome neighbor to all that chose to get in his way. Whenever any of the lighter footed would discover their close proximity to his Appollo pedestals, like a shooting star they would flit away, and leave him monarch of all he surveyed.

I wish to describe a few of the most conspicuous, but I will wait for a quadrille, where I can get them to take their places in description.

The name of my valet de place is Oscar.

"Oscar, what nation does that puny looking, red-skinned

man belong to?" "A *Maltese,*" said he, as if he never would stop sounding the ese, but he added the "I believe." I afterwards found out that he was some of the Canary Island's stock; but the best of the stock. A beautiful French girl held him by the hind part of his coat with her left hand, whilst she held with her right his hand, lest he might go off in his glee, "half shot." She was also afraid that some interested lady might take better care of him than herself. He was fashionably dressed, and in Paris, as a nabob, His actions represented some rich man's foolish son.

I swear by my father's head, I see a live Turk! Turban! sack hanging between his legs, more empty than Falstaff's! one of the genuine breed that followed Saladin to the plains of Palestine and stood before Richard's battle-axe with his scimitar! one of the head choppers of Christians! Perhaps the next will be the amiable countenance of "Blue Beard." The old Turk and his beard is trying to dance, but his bag won't let him. He is let down, and goes off the track. He is now mixing some oakum with tobacco. Now he is looking on, like a poor boy at a frolic — yes! he would if he could I am sure his first duty to-morrow will be to hunt a mosque and give up dancing. He is leaving and trying to get his money back.

I walked round on the opposite side, and saw several other incomprehensibles. "What tall, fine looking, yellow skinned man is that, Oscar, with that tall lady standing

---

Saladin . . . scimitar!: Dorr seems to be using Saladin of Damascus from the European-Muslim wars, or Crusades as they were called, to introduce the Turk in a typically Eurocentric manner. As is also often the case in Dorr's writing, he follows this lighthearted Eurocentric narration with an equally lighthearted racial subversion in which he compares Mr. Cordevoille, a quadroon from Louisiana, with Prince Albert.

Richard: Richard I (1157–1199), king of England, one of the leaders of the Third Crusade. He and Saladin figure in much chivalric literature, including Walter Scott's *Talisman.*

Blue Beard: Character in a tale by Perrault (with an oriental setting) who serially murders his wives.

looking on ?" "That, sir," said he, "is a very rich quadroon from Louisiana, I believe New Orleans. He lives at No. 4, *Boulevard Possoniere*, when he is in town, but he has his country residence nine miles in the country. He has a very handsome French lady for a wife, and it is said he left New Orleans on account of their prejudice to color. He is a very popular man here, and is said to be worth $150,000. Just then I saw Mr. Holbrook, of the New Orleans Picayune, and Mr. Fellowes of the firm of Fellowes & Co., step up to this man and shake him warmly by the hand, and said, "Mr. Cordevoille, don't you know me? I patronized your tailor's shop five or six years." Cordevoille had been the largest tailorizer in the South, and accumulated a large fortune, and sold out to his partner, Mr. Lacroix, who still is carrying on the firm under the name and style of Cordevoille & Lacroix. Mr. Cordevoille was looking the very picture of a gentleman ; he seemed to be a great object of respect to those that spoke to the lady he was conversing with in the French tongue. He reminded me more of Prince Albert in his manners than any other person around. Had his face not been pock marked, he would have conveyed a conception of an inferior Appollo; his *tout ensemble* had as many brilliant cuts of a true gentleman's conduct, as the single diamond he wore. After some enquiry about New Orleans, he invited some American gentlemen to his country seat ; it was to be on the following day, and they being high toned gentlemen of sense, they

---

tout ensemble: Literally "all together"; here it means his complete appearance.

accepted, not so much for pleasure and information, as for
giving Mr. Cordevoille to understand that they understood
the duty of gentlemen; no doubt they felt that if they
refused, Mr. Cordevoille might feel the weight of such a
refusal. They agreed also to stay all night, which invitation
had been extended by Mr. Cordevoille. Lest it be a censure on these gentlemen, I refrain from going any further
with a subject so delicate.

I now walked under the roof of a very extensive hall; in
it was all kinds of refreshments. All one side of the hall
was a door, so that when the crowd in the garden was likely
to be overtaken by a shower, dancing went on in there.
Immense crowds were seated about at tables smoking, and
discussing politics, but not one gentleman had his foot on
the table, except an American quietly seated in one corner
in a profound soliloquy. He was chewing tobacco. I did'nt
stop to see where he spit, for fear he might claim nationality.
I learned that several of the quietly seated, were members
of the National Assembly. It was now getting late,
and gentlemen that had pretty mates were going through
the gates in compact succession. Why gentlemen with
pretty mates could not stay to the last was a mystery
to me. But to solve that mystery I followed the crowd,
and discovered that the nearer they got home, the more
affectionate they got.

The most of these couples would stop at the first
cafe and call for their *tass du coffee* and *vere d'eau de vie*

(cup of coffee and glass of brandy). They would set the brandy on fire and burn the spirits out, and then pour it into the coffee. As soon as they began to feel the effects of this pleasant nourishment, they would move again for home.

At 11 o'clock at night carriages were running in all directions from Balls, Theatres, Operas, Museums, Concerts, Soirees, Dancing Schools, and more amusements than could be named in one article.

I went to the hotel, seeking my own amusement. I could not conjecture a more comfortable place than the house I roomed at, after seeing all this night's bustle. Even if I could not find my own room, I was in the house of acquaintances.

I went to the room of an acquaintance, and talked and lingered in agreeable conversation and amusement until near day. I approached my own chamber, and found that whilst I was out helping to make a city of dissipators, Elvereta had been to my room and arranged my wardrobe *comme foi*. This ends my "first night in Paris."

---

comme foi: The correct French expression is *comme il faut*, which means "just so." Dorr is using phonetic French here.

I MUST ROVE AWAY FROM PARIS.

HERE is the middle of August, nearly a month of unin-
terrupted sight seeing has passed away, and my curiosity is
surfeited.   I am now on the eve of roving away to
" the hilly Oberland," where I will tire my limbs on the
rocky Alps, and crave the comfort I here have enjoyed.
I know I am but leaving Paris to enjoy the anxiety to get
back.

Four days are gone by, and I have spent half a day at
Chalon, and one at Lyons, the "silk city."   In this last
half a day, I saw more manufactories than I ever saw in
one town.   It is said that machines to the enormous power
of two hundred horse, are in some of these factories.
From 50 to 60,000 hands are engaged in manufacturing
silk daily.   This is a very rich looking city, and must
indeed, be very rich.   It is no doubt an older city than
Paris.   If a man was brought here blindfolded, after
beholding its magnificence and wealth, he might easily be
led to believe he was at the Capitol of France.

Another day is gone, and finds me not less fleeting.   I
am away up the Rhone, at " *Aix le Bain*."   This romantic
little town of a few thousand inhabitants, has the celebrity
of chronology of 700 years before the Christian era.   It

points to some warm baths, which it is named after, as its grey hairs; and of which was its phœnix. The Romans built it up on account of its feasibility of becoming a "national bath tub" of Gaul. Under the ground, as far as the ambition of a Roman chooses to go, these baths could be made profitable. There are now from eight to ten stone walled rooms, where all a man has to do to put the bath in readiness, is to open the door.

Some 200 or 300 Frenchmen were here passing away the summer, enjoying themselves fishing, dancing and gaming, for there is a very rich bank in a splendid Casino, to draw that class of France that live on excitement, I saw one American here who was broke. He wanted to relate his misfortunes to me, but I did not wish to hear them, as I was well posted before he tried to post me.

I am intercepted on all sides, as I step off the steps of the hotel, by donkey boys, who are indeed anxious to have me take a ride to a little old city not far away, but in Savoy. It is impossible to tell a good donkey from a bad one by his looks, and each boy assures me that his donkey is the best in Aix. By way of proving it to me, he gives me the word of an American that rode him the summer before; but were I an Englishman instead of what he took me to be, he would have had other testimonials more influential. But what these little good natured plagues say is true, so far as the words of their patrons are to be trusted; it would be very indecorous to ride his little donkey three or four miles, and have the little owner to run along behind all the time and whip and beat the poor donkey, and then get off and walk in without saying he was a "good donkey," "the best you ever saw." That pleases the little fellows. His donkey is worth 5 or $6, and to run down his little stock, would be no part of a gentleman.

August is not yet gone, but I am a long way from Paris. Here I am, at the "City of Watches," Geneva, and lake Leman. Never did a better opportunity present itself to man, to make a good impression, than this beautiful day presents Geneva to me, her visitor. Not a cloud intervenes to Mount Blanc's snow clad peak, fifty odd miles away, and it looks as if it was merely over yonder hill, to the right of Byron's house, which is not two miles away. It reminds me of a still cloud, over a sun-set that indicates fair weather to-morrow. As Mount Blanc is covered with snow here in August,, it makes another mountain of a lesser height that lies between here and Mount Blanc, appear as if its top was painted red. Mount Blanc, standing beyond, with her white capped peak, through the intervening heat of this hot day, the small one may well resemble a fiery painted mountain. This is the edge of Switzerland, and still the French is the prevalent language, which language seems destined to be universal throughout Europe.

After looking over some of the watch factories, I went to Mount Blanc on horses, and stayed two days at the a city at its base, and went across the country to Vevey, a small town on lake Leman. To my astonishment I saw two Americans here. One was Dr. Elliot, of Louisville, Ky., and the other Mr. N., of New Orleans. The old Dr. was very glad to see me. He and I had been sick companions together on the steamship Africa, where and when we both wished that we had never heard of Europe, but now that we were out of the slough, and traveling over the Republican land of Wm. Tell in the very best health and spirits, and like the roe and buck, we were happy in these Highlands.

Vevey is a very handsomely situated village, one would not forget it after seeing its picturesque groups of vine-yards and rustic huts, interspersed with fairy-like palaces. It is a lively little place, and a great many English and rich Switzers come here in the dog days of summer.

After staying at Vevey a couple of days, I hired a car-riage and plodded on over this hilly land to Switzerland's Capital, Bern. Bern is a very dull looking place, and most especially so for a Capitol. The second story of the houses hang over the pavement, so you can walk the town with-out getting wet. The language generally is German, so you see the close alliance of languages in Switzerland.

Five days more; I am in the Great Oberland, among the towering Alps. I traversed the whole of the valley of Interlaken, to the almost hidden village of Interlaken. The hotels are all small, generally not more than ten rooms, and are called pensions; queer name to create an appetite with.

English come here in summer for cheap living; there is also some Americans with patience enough to stay a short time and strengthen their means, that are most too frequently consumed at Paris, Brussels, or Vienna. As you leave the village to take a tour in a carriage up the great valley, you pass the ruins of an ancient castle, which once was the court of an ancient and noble race, whose ancestors are not to be traced, whose names was Unspunnin. A young knight belonging to another court scaled the walls, and stole away Ida, the last male descendant's daughter, and made her his bride. Many years of bloody strife followed, after which the young knight came forth to Burkard, the lord of this castle and father of Ida, with his infant son in his arms and offered himself up, when the old man went into tears and made Rudolph's infant son heir of his numerous estates.

Farther up the valley a place is pointed out where a great murder was committed, and a noble young knight was the doer of the deed. He could never rest afterwards, so he fled from the sight of man, and has never been heard of since. In the immense vallies of perpetual glaciers, the snow has lain for thousands of years, and where the mountains drip upon the glaciers below, crevasses are made through and under. It is supposed that this knight crept into one of these and there froze up his heart, unseen by father, mother, sister, brother, friend or acquaintance.

This part of Switzerland is unlike any other part. It is nothing but mountains and small lakes. The lakes are as apt to be found on the tops of mountains as in vallies. From these large basins of water on top of mountains, are crevasses running through side rocks, and falling off makes the crevasses through and under the glaciers as I have described.

But here is a specimen of the intelligence of the Switzers of olden time. It is a little old town with a wall round it, and a hill close up to the wall all round. The walls could have done no more good than the hill if there was any spunk in the builders. The lake of Lucern comes up to this bigoted little spot. Its appelation is in honor of this important lake of catfish and suckers. It has a piece of art, too, a lion sculptured in the side of a rock outside the walls. It is the most natural artificial lion I ever saw. Here is Zurich, the prettiest city in Switzerland, notwithstanding Byron's praise of Geneva. Here is the famed "Zurich waters." The people here have not that staring stupidity so characteristic of the Swiss in other towns. They are all going along about their business as if they had lived among strangers all their lives. It is a thriving town, and they manufacture silks here on quite an extensive scale. In conclusion, Switzerland is a Republic, and all parts, except the ruggedest mountains, is in the highest state of cul-

tivation.   Wine and wheat are among their chief studies.
They are devout christians.   Every mile of their highways
there is an image of the Son of Mary hung high up by the
roadside, denoting his suffering, patience and forbearance.
The Swiss are not a homely people.   Their country is too
mountainous for railroads.

SPICY TOWNS IN GERMANY.

HAVING passed over the borders of Switzerland and Germany, and through the first German town, called Friedsburg, I will linger a while at Strasborg. It was once the Capitol of many provinces. In times gone by, many centuries ago, it was called the Roman's " Argentoratum," and experienced more than a few of the miseries of war. The tallest piece of monumental art the world ever had recorded on the pages of its Chronology, not even the Tower of Babel excepted, is here in this city of over two thousand years old. Its name is the Munster, and ought to have been Monster. It is a Church, and was three hundred years in process of erection. It is 474 feet from the earth, and to give a clearer perception of its height, it is 24 feet higher than the Pyramids of Egypt. In it is that famous clock, made three hundred years ago, which runs yet. This clock might justly have an other half added to its name, *clock*. Many people flock there every day to see its manœuvres. At 12 o'clock, or a few minutes before twelve, wooden men, representing the Apostles or Priests, come out of the clock, and some inferior personages also, and march a short distance and waits a few minutes to be warned of the hour, then this waited for moment is signalized by a brass cock coming out of the clock on the other side, which flaps its wings three times and crows, after which this group of old men returns to their vestry of study or seclusion, and the clock clicks on as it has done for three hundred years, and the crowd disperses.

The streets are crowded with soldiers, as in Paris, and the ladies go about the streets holding up their dresses just the right height to attract attention.

The rain is over, and there is no more attraction in the spicy town of Strasborg, so I am going to Baden Baden, the spiciest gambling place in Europe. In the Park is a great large building in the shape of a country stable, but full of splendor, called a Casino or conversation room, and this conspicuous appellation is conspicuously written on the front of the building. In this open hall—open to all—is gambling hours between each meal. The great gambling table is in the centre with numerous stools, such as are to be found in Stuarts, or any other fashionable Dry Goods store in America. On these stools are all classes of society that like excitement — dukes, earls, marquises, barons, knights, valets, and even liveried coachmen, betting from 5 francs to 10,000 francs. While I was in the Casino the Prince of Prussia broke the bank. Only thirty thousand francs is allowed in the Bank at once, and if broken no more business or amusement goes on that day in that Cassino; but there are others dealing on the same platform.

It is quite amusing to see the anxiety written on the brow
of players, and to see the expression of disinterested persons, which we in America term "stuck on the game." I
have seen more excruciating pain come from an outsider by
the loss of some pile of gold, than I ever saw come from the
expression of the loser. Here comes a Count who has been
betting and losing on another bank, and he came to change
his luck. He threw down his last thousand and it won;
he let it all stand on the red, and this time it all goes into
the bank. He exclaims, "that's my luck." Then the
outsiders would cast an eye of pity on him, and say, he
might have known that he would lose it, when the very
reason they were not betting, was, they were broke on the
same bank perhaps a week ago. I see six beautiful noble
ladies betting, with their money snugly piled up before
them. Their bets generally range from twenty to one
hundred francs. But the most amusing part of this crowd's
entertainment is, the airs that the money scampers put on.
If a lady or gentleman should win, he pays it with an air
of nonchalence and great pleasure; but if he wins, which
he is sure to do in the end, he looks very melancholy, as if
it were the result of accident, and in his opinion it was very
vulgar for the bank to win. I put down a five franc piece,
it won; I let the ten stand, it won; I let the twenty stand,
it won; I moved it, and it lost, and I quit. He attempted
to console me by saying I ought to have let it stand where
it was, "what do you bet on now sir," said he; I don't bet

any more said I, I have already lost five francs. He took me to be a green Yankee and said no more to me. Another amusing sight was there; it was two more broken American youths, who said they were waiting for Mr. Peabody to forward them money, and was " sound on the borry." I did'nt pride myself much here on my nationality, lest I would have some unprofitable fame. One of them owed two weeks' board in the British Hotel. He was mighty polite when he met me in company, and placed me under the truly painful necessity of being introduced to some person of note whom he had himself been a bore upon. He asked me if I was acquainted with the Grand Duke, at the same time looking over the heads of the players, as if he would call him if he could only get his eye on him. Then he insisted on my going down to the other Bank, where the chances were better. and where the Grand Duke of Baden would most likely be. I declined all invitations, and got a carriage and went out of town to see the ruins of the Erhreinstein Castle.

Having returned and paid my bill, I left this little German town to go to Heidelburg, where once dwelled a good Castilian, Frederick the 1st, of the Palatinate.

James lived between Baden Baden and Heidelberg two or three years, and wrote the two following novels, which gives a better history of these, the Castles of Heidelberg and Erhreinstein, than any other history gives or can be obtained at present. He lived at Carlsruth. The Grand

---

Frederick the 1st, of the Palatinate: Emperor Frederick Barbarossa of the German kingdom: he ruled from 1152 to 1190.

Duke lives at Baden Baden, and Carlsruth, and Heidelberg, and he is here now at Heidelberg, and was here when my American friend was hunting him in the Casino.

Tilly, the great French general, blew up the front side of this castle in 1620, since which all its magnificence has been known but as tradition. The picture gallery still remains perfect, that is to say, some wings of it. There is many talented artists now grouped about in its rural halls, for the grass has grown up in them, taking copies of these splendid pictures. The city of Heidelberg which this castle overlooks, is quite a large city for a German interior town. I was told by my landlord that its population was upwards of 60,000. The cellar of the old ruins still contains its wine casks. I saw one cask or vat said to hold 60,000 bottles of wine. Ten men can dine round a King Arthur's round table on its head. In the cellar is the statue of one of King Frederick's fools, with one side of his face painted green and one half of his hair red, whilst the other is not. He drank eighteen bottles of wine each day and lived one hundred years. Father Matthew never heard of that juice of such admirable longevity, or it would have clapped the cap on his spouting eloquence. German towns are spicy towns. Outside of the city, just across the necker, is to be two duels to-day with short swords, and they fight duels on that duelling ground every day, either students or other citizens. It is considered a small gladiatorial arena. The Grand Duke is about to leave for Carlsruth, and the people

---

Tilly, the great French general: Johan Tserclaes, count of Tilly (1559–1632), commander of the army of the Catholic League and later of the imperial army during the Thirty Years' War. Tilly was mortally wounded in a battle against Gustavus Adolphus of Sweden in 1632.

are parading with great glee. Children women and men are crowding the gates in solid batallions; you would think old Zack had come to town.

I am dizzy with reflections of these fast little towns of Germany. As I whirl along now towards the cradle of the Rothschild's my brain is rocking its reflective matter from the canton of the quiet and religious Swiss here to the burghers of this profane people. But here I am, in the independent little territory of the Duchess of Darmstadt. Each mile-post is painted barber-pole style. This Duchess is better known as the Duchess of Nassau. The cars stopped at Darmstadt, and if a good big southern barber's shop had been here the people all would have gone in it instead of Darmstadt by mistake. The gates are barberified in its style of designation.

I saw an American looking out of the cars at these posts until he felt his beard. All at once he threw himself back in his seat, as if he thought the country was too dull to look at, and of course impossible to produce anything sharp enough to take off beards.

Frankfort may be strictly termed the capitol of Germany; because all the German Princes meet here once a year and hold a conference on the great topics of interest to the whole German people. This gathering is called the Diet This Diet enacts for the German principalities, some of the most wholesome and sound logical laws that comes from the parliament of any nation of these modern times. Frankfort

---

cradle of the Rothschild's: famous banking family of the nineteenth century headed by Meyer Amschel Rothschild in Frankfurt. Rothschild's sons went to London, Paris, and Vienna and set up different branches of their banks. The Rothschilds were one of the richest families in Europe in the nineteenth century.

Duchess of Darmstadt: Darmstadt was one of the states that made up the German confederation. Germany was divided into twenty-three states until 1871.

has produced the most sagacious merchants the world ever knew. I have just been to look at Goethe's house. It has stood the scathing weather of the main for five hundred years, but none of the calamities of time have laid their fingers upon it, save a slight decay.

"Frankfort on the Oder" must not be misconstrued so as to convey an idea of this Frankfort. This is generally designated as Frankfort on the Main. It is a town full of high spirited people, and lively as crickets, but less sedate. Business is always good here. Each man is in some degree possessed with the ambition of a Rothschild. I am going to see the house of the primitive Rothschild, and then off to the Rhine.

Here I am at Mainz, on the banks of the Rhine. Looking at my ticket down the Rhine, I see this is the 17th of September, but the weather indicates summer time. This old, dead, but vast town, has the distinction allotted to it of producing the first book printer.

I will not attempt, as most chroniclers, to describe the impression the legend river of Europe made on me; suffice it to say that, on every peak, and that is saying a good deal, is the ruins of tyrants, and every hole that is made through these turrets, sends out a woeful wisp of a "Blue Beard's wrath," that quickens the pulse of a modern civilian.

I am now in town, at a great hotel, called Disch. Here is a very old city, and in old times Roman emperors were

---

Goethe: Johann Wolfgang Goethe, famous German writer (1749–1832). His best-known work, *Faust*, was published in 1808.

proclaimed here. The wife of Germanicus, Aggrippa, the mother of the tyrant that "fiddled" whilst Rome was burning, was born here. In this city is a church which has already cost four millions of florins, and is not finished yet. In this church is one of the most imposing pieces of splendor the eye of man ever gazed on. Inside of this case of jewels is three skulls filled with jewels. They glitter about in the nose and eyes and ears like moving maggots, and causes man to gaze with amazement upon the peculiarities of thepeople of German towns. Its name is Cologne. Its modern merit is its production of Colognes, not little towns, but the fluid possessing requisite qualifications of admittance to the private apartment of the sweetest virgin.

I must now bring this chapter to a close and go down among the Dutch.

The wife of Germanicus, Aggrippa: This casual reference makes a few errors. Agrippa was a Roman general who lived from 63 to 12 B.C. His daughter, Agrippina, was the wife of Germanicus. Her daughter, Agrippina the Younger (15–59 A.D.), was the mother of "the tyrant" Nero.

DOWN AMONG THE DUTCH.

HAVING been disappointed in seeing a magnificent city, and smelling one, I am rapidly running down the Rhine to the Netherlands—Holland among the Dutch. These boats are hardly worth mentioning, more than to say they have steam and a crew. The crew are very stupid looking; mind you I say stupid looking, but I don't mean to say they are stupid. They have nothing to say or do with the passengers. They don't leave their watch and come to the cabin to sit a minute and talk with passengers, and occasionally "take a hand" at a game, as they do on our inferior boats running the Yazoo, Arkansas, Red and Black River, until the boiler hisses, or the boat snags. They are slow but sure.

In the cabin, which is below, is a sufficient number of small tables in restaurant style, and whoever eats does it *a la carte*. If you eat what is worth only fifteen grochens, you only pay fifteen grochens; but, if you eat one hundred grochens' worth, you will pay one hundred grochens; not one cent over or under is required, for the Dutch, as a class, are a reasonable, just and inoffensive people, therefore wish nothing but fair understanding and dealing. They always keep an interpreter on a cheap scale, to enable them to get along without difficulty. He was either a waiter, dish washer or potato-peeler, but on a no more expensive scale. They are the last people I am acquainted with to count un-hatched chickens.

Captain Husenhork, I understand, is a gentleman and a good humored man, but the eye of a lynx would have a task to catch a smile upon his hickory countenance. He brought an old Dutch musket on deck for me to amuse myself with, shooting at snipe along the dykes. I shot into their midst several times, but they all flew up, circled around and lit at the same place. I never before saw so many of this style or genera of bird. Their bills was the most conspicuous part of them.

The boat is now turning to land at a pretty large town called Arnheim; but Holland is so low that a man cannot see the spires of a city until he enters its walls.

Holland is one vast marsh. It is dyked so as to drain each acre, but it is the richest soil in Europe, and its productiveness is so profitable that its owners would not swop it for the land of Goshen. It has nourished a people that seem to be well adapted to its nature; the forbearance of the Dutch people is not to be equalled by any. The labor required to till such soil as Holland's, has been the best friend to the Hollanders, for no people on the earth enjoys the labor as does a Holland farmer, and no people

could make it so profitable. In taking a hack ride a few
miles in the country around Arnheim, I can say the nur-
series are unsurpassed by Switzerland, the Hanse States, or
France.

Having gossiped in Arnheim two days, I called for my
bill, paid it, packed my trunk for Amsterdam. Wine being
such an extravagant item I thought I would enquire into it,
as I might get some information why it was so much more
in Holland than the other parts of the Rhine. I found that
wine was an imported liquor, consequently, the duty made
the difference between wine on that side of the Rhine and
the other. A swilly beer is most universally the bevarage
of the Netherlands. The clerk supposing that I was not
satisfied with the length of my bill, took it in his inspection
and examined it carefully, and said, "Sir, you eat snipe."
"Well is that any reason you should make my bill like a
snipes?" "Yes sir," said he, "it is extra." "All right,
sir, I did not ask you about any part of the bill except
wine." Next day I was in Amsterdam, the wealthiest city
of Holland. It is a city of canals ; they run through all
the main parts of the town, leaving a large side-walk on
each side. Some pretty large ships are in the heart of the
town. Bridges run across the canals, but they revolve on
hinges and are easily turned.

The gayest time of Amsterdam is dead winter. Then the
Zuyder Zee and all its canals are frozen over, when ladies
and gentlemen are skating night and day. Vessels sail

charmingly on the ice, but their bottoms are made for the
ice instead of water. Balls and pic-nic parties are numerous
in winter. The Amsterdam ladies are all healthy looking.
I saw half a dozen ladies yesterday shooting snipe, when I
rode out to Saandam. They had on nice little boots and
moved among the high grass like skilful hunters. At Saandam I registered my name in the little "book of names," in
the house of Peter the Great, Emperor of Russia. He ran
away from Russia and came here and rented this little house
with only two rooms, and lived in poverty here, to learn to
build ships. Hollandaise builders worked with him a year
at a time, but knew not that it was Peter the Great, of the
Russias. The little frame hut is three hundred years old,
but has been preserved on account of its strange and novel
history.

26th of September, and I am at the capitol of Holland,
The Hague. The King lives here, about a quarter of a mile
from my hotel, the "Bellevue." But I just dined with a
King. The father of the Queen is the old King of Wurtem-
burg, and he is putting up here, and we have a guard of
honor at our door. He is going out—he bows to me.

COL. FELLOWES LEARNING DUTCH.

I MUST now introduce the reader to an American "merchant Prince," better known by his associates as the "Prince of Good Fellows." This is Cornelius Fellowes, of the respectable firm of Messrs. Fellowes & Co., of New Orleans, La. He is rather more than a medium size man, and straight as an exclamation point, with handsome limbs. He cannot be justly termed handsome, without adding *man*. His face was the color of a last year's red apple all free from decay; his hair is light for black, and not very thick on top, and he is aged 48 years. He is no politician, statesman, or orator, but as a business man, he is "sound on the goose." I know of no man that could settle business disagreements to the entire satisfaction of both, better than Mr. Fellowes. He would have made a profound judge, his heart and talent alike is so justly qualified. He is a very liberal and extravagant man, more so than any man I am acquainted with, but he is by no means a benevolent man; I don't mean to say that he is stingy, for he is not, but I mean to indicate

---

He is rather more than a medium size . . . 48 years: This description (and the entire chapter) is an example of Dorr's radical critique and understated style. Dorr describes Fellowes's body as if Fellowes were a slave at auction by does not explicitly make the analogy.

that he always has some original idea of his own to make him give ; for example, if a group of little ragged girls come around him begging, he will instantly feel his pockets, and take out all the change, but the most of it would go into the hands of the prettiest or cleanest, at the same time saying, "this is a pretty little girl," and if there is any left they will be sure to get the remainder. Or if a group of little boys are the beggars, he will give the most to the smartest, and exclaim, "he is a smart little fellow." And sometimes he is conscious of this partiality, and tries to evade it by throwing the coin among the boys to see them scuffle for it, but this trait of his is so marked, that he will be sure to throw it on his favorite's head, and if he fails to catch it, it is a sure sign of another chance for the boys. He laughs heartily when his boy catches it, as if it done his soul good. He is so proud, or haughty, or perhaps I had better say, naturally aristocratic, that he can descend from his sphere to vulgar without knowing it, and joke, laugh, and even offer some of his drink, but if you forget yourself, he will recollect himself. He can treat a free colored man as polite as he can a poor white one, and a class that are below them must be in his estimation what they are.

He is a man with no enemies ; I don't believe he has one, and he himself hates no man, and in fact is always happy, jovial, and scarcely ever disappointed with his calculations of things and people. Whatever the Col. does,

he does well, but he always puts it off until it can be delayed
no longer. If he makes up his mind that he must go
up the river, and look in the affairs of his agents or
debters, he will appoint next week, but four or five weeks
will follow in succession, but as next week must eventually
come, he battles with that until the last day. Saturday he
leaves on the last boat, and, is his most interested partner
abler than another man to tell when he will ever turn his
face home, or whether he will stop at Natchez, or Memphis,
for what convinced him at 2 o'clock Saturday that he had
better get off that evening, was as much the departure of his
friends on that boat, as the conviction that these affairs of
his must be looked into. When he wants a partner in any
of his various traffics, he never looks for a man with capital,
but one that understands what his views are, and would feel
an aspiring interest, so much so as to devote all his time
and talent and scrutiny to its developement of prosperity in
the end, if not at first. His object seems more the perfection
of the business than its profits; but at the end of the year
of business, which is the first day of September, if there is
no profit, and he is not very deeply in, he will not be inclined
to risk much, but he sticks like a leech, and this year must
pay the loss of last. He will bleed some branch of this
business before he lets go. The balance sheet of the firm
of Messrs. Fellowes and Co., foots per annum about
$140,000. to $170,000 profit; but if he lost by giving up
some of his planters that have made a good crop, $10,000,

he thinks that he managed badly, and goes about finding
who they are connected with, and whether they wish to
come back again. He will now furnish them with more
means than he refused them when they left him. No man
can get along with a planter better than Cornelius Fellowes;
for he considers a planter, or slave holder, his equal in every
particular; consequently feels himself at home with them.
A planter looks at a merchant as his agent until they become
the leading houses in their community, then they are
honored in having the great merchant to stay a few days
and hunt. But when they go to New Orleans they
expect to be waited on by the merchant, when to their great
disgust, the merchant sends his clerk to look after their
wants; and the merchant, instead of persuading them to
come and put up at his house, or dine with him, has other
friends more congenial to his taste and dignity, than the
planter with his Sunday suit of store made clothes. But as
Mr. Fellowes never cares much for looks or position, and as
he is an old bachelor and never had a house, and a slave
holder is his equal, he hesitates not to go to the ladies
ordinary and order his seat at table, and call on the rustic
gentleman and family to dine with him, where they drink
such wine as they would most likely take at home for stump
water and cider. But this familiarity will tell upon the
nerves of Mr. Fellowes, for he does not like to feel himself
obliged to do any thing, and they will, in this good mood,
invite him to the opera, theatre, or most likely the circus.

Now this stumps his benevolent feelings to those who need
no benevolence; he has his club mates, or the gaieties of
Orleans to meet, where are to be found the very men he
must touch glasses or whif a cigar with. He is now puzzled.
He will let them know before dark, but will have their
tickets for them already. He surely will be found missing;
he says to himself "it will not do to refuse them without a
good and plausable excuse," therefore he plans in his mind.
He calls on one of his numerous clerks, and requests him to
take an amount of money and go and buy so many tickets,
and requests him further to call on Mr. Brown, and make
an excuse, and offer to accompany him and the ladies to the
amusement in view. These rich, bustle-dressed, young
girls are diamonds in the eyes of young clerks; and young
clerks in the best houses arc Adonises to what these girls
are used to. They soon become agreeable, and when they
return home, Sam Smith, their next neighbor, is treated as
he deserves to be by civilized beings. Soon after a letter
comes to Mr. Clerk from this plantation, with a lady's scrawl,
care Fellowes & Co., and Mr Fellowes delights to find that
his suggestion of this young man met the entire approbation
of the favorite of the old farmer. The fact is Mr. Fellowes
can kill more birds with one stroke of his policy, than any
other man that studies so little. Mr. Fellowes is never in
so bad a humour as when he treats one kindly, and it is
unkindly returned, to illustrate this, I must drop this epitome
of his history, and carry the reader to the Capitol of Holland,

where Mr. Fellowes is trying to learn something of this slow
and easy people. He was smoking his segar when the King
of Wurtimburg went out, but took no notice of him, because
he was engaged with a group of beggar boys, throwing
stivers at them. An English gentleman that had lived in
the Indies, was by us, and we had travelled on the Rhine
together. "Let us go down to the sea, five miles off, and
see the Dutch fisheries. I understand they are extensively
engaged in fishing, Mr. Grant," said Col. Fellowes. "I
have been there, Mr. Fellowes," said the Englishman, "but
will go again with you, though I know you will be annoyed
with these plagued beggars." "O," said Mr. Fellowes, "I
like to see them, with their large wooden shoes, jumping
after the grochens, and further, they are a great people, and
I wish to find out a great deal about their habits and manners; I think I shall stay here a week." The fame of the
Col. had reached the remotest corner of the Hague, and
squads of two and three were seen in all directions coming
to the Bellevue House. Here our lacquey brought before
the door a fine turnout, and he jumped in and drove away
like a prince, whilst they followed on all sides, some
hundreds of yards, like Fallstaff's soldiers, ready to run
from any one they found they were close to that knew them
except their abject leader. In a few moments we were down
on the North sea. It was very cold down on the beach, but
fishermen were walking in the sea from their smacks, with
hamper baskets full of all kinds of fish. Their vessels

Wurtimburg: Württemberg, region of southwest Germany, a kingdom
from 1813 to 1918.
Fallstaff [*sic*]: See note to p. 27.

that had been two days seining, was full of fish, but as these vessels could get no nearer than a quarter of a mile to land, they always fill their bushel basket, and shoulder it, and walk through the surging waves on the beach, on whose sand was pyramids of fish piled up, to be sold at a zwanzich bushels (about 25 cents). Sometimes they would disappear in the waves with the fish, but would appear soon again nearer shore, plodding on patiently.

Whilst Col. Fellowes was reading a description of this fish point, the lacquey explained a conversation he had with six or seven beggars off a rod from us. He said they were anxious to know who we three fellows were, and had dubbed Mr. Fellowes "Count of New York." I was son of the Count, and would eventually become Count of the Amsterdam, of the Empire state. Mr. Grant was dignified with the royal appellation of "Duke of Brunswick." They certainly found more curious matter in the polish of our glazed boots, than we did at their large wooden trotters, that at every step rattled against the others, who stood so close together as to form a bouquet of dirty Dutch heads of various colors.

Having informed Mr. Fellowes of his new made honor, he laughed heartily, and called them nearer to corroborate the information that they had been so lucky to find out, by throwing among them some of his revenue of the city named after their great Amsterdam. The Col. threw stavers and grochens until he astonished the natives. Some

jumped clear over other's heads. Now the Col. was in his
glory. This was Friday, and they had'nt eaten anything.
but from their movements and agility, you would swear "they
would make hay while the sun shines."   Their strange
movements was not only a signal for miles up the beach, but
the fishermen had abandoned their smacks, and were coming
through the surf, and under it.   The Col. here run out of
money, and called on my money bag, which was hanging
under my arm like a bird bag, and was full of various coins,
from Louis d' Or's of twenty franc pieces, to the smallest
denominations.   I gave small coin until I thought he had
thrown away enough, and then cried broke. Mr. Grant
and myself drew back from the Col., and he was beseiged.
He told them he was broke, at the sams time feeling all his
pockets, whilst they was looking all around him for pockets
he might overlook.   About sixty or seventy had circled
him, and we were laughing to ourselves because we saw he
was vexed and felt himself in a dilemna.   The little Dutch
had almost fell down in the sand by his feet, and was feeling
up his pantaloons leg to see if some was not dropping.   One
old honest Dutchman that had been carefully examining
Mr. Fellowes coat tail, had come across his white handkerchief, and took it round in front and returned it.   Here Mr.
Fellowes showed tokens of fear, and he hallowed out,
"Lacquey, why don't you take a stick and beat them off,
don't you see they are robbing me?"   "No sir, that
handkerchief he thought was something that you had

overlooked sticking to your clothes, and he brought it to
your notice," said the lacquey. "Then tell them I am
broke and drive them off." "Yes, sir, if I can. Here he
went to work in earnest, explaining that the Count had run
out of money but he had a plenty in the Bank, and they
could get no more to-day. Then they went away about a
rod and seemed buried in reflection. They started to come
again, but the Col. backed, while the lacquey appealed to
their reason by informing them that were it the king himself, he could not carry all his money with him. Mr. Fellowes shook himself and tried to put on a pleasing countenance, but we could not for our lives maintain our gravity
at his lesson of familiarity while learning Dutch.

We walked up the beach, and conversed on the subject
of the North Sea and Sir John Franklin, when all of a
sudden Mr. Fellowes called to the coachmon to drive up.
I looked around and saw the beggars coming. We lost
no time in retreating. While passing through the gates of
the city, I noticed a bronze lion placed in the position of a
guardian over it. I said, what an awful condition Daniel
must have been in when in the lion's den. "No worse,"
said the Col. "than I was in with the Dutch!" Here a
boy opened a door on the Col.'s side, that he might descend. As the Col. stepped out, he alighted on the Dutchman's wooden shoe, and tripped himself up. As he picked
himself up and moved towards the hotel door, he exclaimed
in an under tone, d———n the Dutch.

It must not be supposed that Mr. Fellowes meant any harm to the Dutch, but, they were not in his opinion, as agreeable as they might be.   He left next day, although he intended staying a week "learning Dutch."

ON! ON! TO WATERLOO.

WITHOUT noting Rotterdam, Holland's lowest town, and Antwerp, an old Flemish town, I am at the carpet city of Belgium, Brussels, on my way to Waterloo. I have a little old lacquey I just hired and he is as cute as a mink. "All ready, sir," said he, "shall I drive you to the Palace or the Museum?" No sir, on to Waterloo!" Here the hackman remonstrated—he was not engaged for twelve miles and only engaged inside the city walls, and would not go to Waterloo this cold wet day for less than twenty francs. "Go on, sir," said I, and he traversed the whole of the Brussels Boulevard before he passed the gates. Here we are at the battle-field where Wellington rose and Napoleon fell. Wellington conquered the master of the world. Byron says, in his Ode on Napoleon,—

> " 'Tis done! but yesterday a king,
>   And armed with kings to strive ;
>   And now thou art a nameless thing—
>   So abject, yet alive "

He continues:—

> " Is this the man with thousand thrones
>   Who strewed our earth with hostile bones,
>   And can he yet survive ?
>   Since he miscalled the morning star,
>   Nor man nor fiend hath fallen so far."

My guide was an old revolutionary soldier who was opposed to the Bourbons before the days of Charles the 10th. He fought in this bloody fray, and pleads up fool play on the part of Grouchy.

Mr. Cotton's clerk sold me a copy of a book giving the details of this battle, which it took ten years to accumulate the matter for. Mr. Cotton was in the battle or close to it. In the centre of this field is now an immense mound, made with the bones of slain warriors. Small steps run up to its top, and Wellington is a monumental emblem seated on a horse moving over the field, apparently as natural as life, pinnacling this mound.

Having rested my body by leaning on the leg of the horse, I listened to the harangue of this old man, whose jaws had crept into his mouth, which was void of teeth. He first pointed out the position of Grouchy, who was not in the battle, but was Napoleon's climaxing reserve, off miles in the distance. He now evidently felt some of the animating spirit of that great day, as, pointing in the same direction, he showed me the hill over which Blucher came, and made Napoleon believe that it was his own

---

revolutionary soldier . . . Charles the 10th: Charles X, king of France from 1824, abdicated in 1830.

Grouchy . . . Blucher: Dorr is recounting events during the battle of Waterloo. Grouchy was the French general under Napoleon whose failure to keep Blücher, the Prussian general, from joining Wellington's forces may have cost Napoleon the battle.

Grouchy. The old man quieted his feelings before proceeding farther. He assured me that Napoleon's heartstrings must have burst at this perfidious conduct of Grouchy. He believed that Grouchy was so angry with Napoleon for refusing to let him lead on the battle in the morning instead of French Generals and Marshals, that he sold himself to the allies. Grouchy was one of Napoleon's German Generals, and wanted the glory of a battle which, if lost, would bankrupt the French nation, as they had drained their coffers to support the ambition of its chief, which, no doubt, was the greatest general of modern times. The old soldier pointed off to the right of Blucher's march over the hill, to the French position of Belle Alliance, and referred to those hours of anxiety from the first evening Napoleon arrived there and saw the English in the distance, when he craved the power of Joshua to stop the sun that he might attack them that day, to the close of the battle, when he mounted his white steed and started to the carnage, that he might fall among the slain, and how he was checked by Marshal Soult, which Marshal is yet living, who said to Napoleon, "They will not slay you but take you prisoner," upon which he fled from the scene of desolation and mourning.

The old soldier now turned languidly round to Hougomont, and there depicted some of the most daring fighting that ever a juvenile ear listened to. He said that Napoleon ordered Hougomont to be taken, and gave so many soldiers

---

Napoleon ordered Hougomont to be taken: An incident during the battle of Waterloo.

for that purpose. Hougomont is a long brick building, like an old fashioned barracks. It has a hedge of tall shrubbery in front, looking towards the battle plain. Thousands of English were stationed there with loop holes only a foot apart, so as to shoot down all attacks. When the French soldiers went towards the house to take it, they were shot down one upon another so fast that the few thousands sent against it were slain before they reached the hedge, where the French thought the fire came from. Word was sent to Napoleon that Hougomont could not be taken, and asking for an answer to the leader. Napoleon glanced once round the field, and said, " Tell him to take Hougomont," but he reinforced the leader, who said to his true soldiers, " Let us march up to die, the emperor says, take Hougomont." When these soldiers heard the orders of their emperor, they scuffled over the hedge to find the fire of their enemy, but to their great disappointment it came from the loopholes ! but these daring veterans were not inclined to disobey the great emperor, who was no more a " little corporal." " They," says history, " marched up to the muzzles of the English muksets, and grappled with them till they sank beneath their wrath." Afterwards they took it, but could not keep it. They took it again and kept it some time, but finally left it in the hands of the enemy.

The old man says there were all sorts of reports on the field the night after the battle concerning the emperor. One was, that he rode into the fight and fell with the old guard, who made a pyramid over his body trying to screen him from the blows which fell on him; others were, that Wellington had him in close confinement, and when this was told, thonsands of mangled men that seemed to be living only to hear his fate, fell back and died the death that none can die but a soldier. Next day the news came to the living wounded, that Napoleon was on his way, if not at Fontainbleau, and the old soldiers sprang up on their broken limbs, and filled the air with *vive l'empereur, vive toujours.*

Blucher and Wellington then commenced preparing to march on Paris and did. Blucher wanted to burn it but Wellington knew the revengeful spirit of the nation. He might have burned Paris as his allies wished, and, like Nero, fiddled while it burned, but all France would have been annihilated, or London razed to the earth.

Napoleon sent to Paris to know the Cabinet's opinion of this awful disaster to her Treasury and dignity. Tallyrand who was at the head of affairs, advised him to stay away from Paris, for he bankrupted France, and therefore, must abdicate. Napoleon sent a faithful man to plead in favor of his son, but Tallyrand said he had cost France millions of souls, besides bankrupting her, and must leave unconditionally.

Next morning this king of a hundred thrones rode out of Fontainbleau towards Dieppe. He went aboard an English vessel and said, "I am Napoleon." The old captain

---

vive l'empereur, vive toujours: Long live the emperor, live forever.

trembled as he saw the resemblance of that cold countenance, whose pictures filled even the hamlets of England. Struck with this importance, he untied his vessel, drew up his sail and steered to the admiral. Thus ends this Chapter as it did Napoleon, whose orders some days ago were, "On to Waterloo."

THE BIAS OF MY TOUR.

HERE is Ghent. It is a large city, and a great many of the Brussells carpets are made here. There is no doubt it is as old a city as London. It is here the famous " Treaty of Ghent " was made by Henry Clay and John Adams. I have just been in their old residence, which, from appearances, must have been one of the best houses in Ghent. A good deal of silk is manufactered here even now. A great many Flemish families live here. The city supports an Operā, besides Theatres and other places of amusement. They are inclined to be Frenchy on the Sabbath. I went on the Sabbath to see a horse go up in a balloon. Three men, who paid a certain sum, took passage with the beast, and as he hung below the balloon, well strapped so he could not kick or agitate himself, these passengers were seated above ; I hated it much, as the beast looked so melancholy and innocent. I had seen the same performance at Paris. It was not such a novelty to the horse as to me, for this was the same horse I had seen at Paris some time before. Away they went, upward like a

---

"Treaty of Ghent": Signed in Ghent, Belgium, on December 24, 1814, this agreement between the United States and Great Britain ended the War of 1812.

cloud, in a hurry toward the sea, and were soon lost to our sight.

Another day is gone and leaves me in Bruges ; an old quiet city that figured much in the romantic affairs of Flanders. Bad hotels are plentiful here, with wise men to keep them, for if a man was to keep them better, he would soon have to keep none. We were the only occupants, or even strangers in town. And as we walked out to see its wonders, we found that our arrival had excited the curiosity of a hundred beggars. It is a characteristic trait of beggars, to keep quiet when they see a stranger in town, like a dog with his bone he wishes the picking of alone. But always betray themselves by waiting too long about the hotel where their victim resides. They generally watch the movement of the shrewdest beggar, and keep in his track. They most always keep themselves concealed from view, until they get their victim fairly launched ; then with the sails of poverty, like boreas, they will follow him up till they drive his temper straight into the channel of charity, where we can only find safety in our acts of humanity. Here I was right for once, because I had procured an immense quantity of the smallest coin. I called them all up, and told the lacquey de place to tell them I would give them all I had, if they would cease to follow us, it was agreed, and I give him about half a pint of small coin to divide among them ; he give it to a responsible n e and they all followed him in counsel.

I said in August on my departure from Paris, that I was leaving it to "enjoy the anxiety to get back." Now I am biasing my tour in verification of that expression. I am now close to Paris, and can go there to night. It is eleven o'clock at night, and I am at Paris. I am going to stay this winter, as I am getting used to the life here. Last night I arrived at the Hotel des Princes; the pretty little portress was glad to see me, and I felt at home. She asked me if I wanted a bottle of water with ice inside; she gave me all the news, and showed me a list of her American occupants, and said the Russian Princess was gone, not from Paris, but to private rooms. I put a five franc piece in her hand to convince her I was the same man in all particulars, and went to my room and looked around for Elverata, who used to arrange my wardrobe so nice and say, with neatness on her brow, "How do you like that, Mr. Dorr?" I did not see her and rang the bell, when a strange waiter came quickly and I enquired for Elverata; he satisfied the enquiry by saying he was only a few days there and could not say. I went to bed. Next morning I saw the shadow of a woman moving towards my drawer, I raised my weary head on my elbow and said, "Good morning, Elverata." The woman quietly passed out; I rose and dressed and went to enquire for unpretending Elverata, but like a plant under the cloud of night, I was seeking a tear, she was dead! and dead only one month, and everybody had forgotten her. I had difficulty in that vast hotel to make them understand who I was seeking. I asked what graveyard she was buried in, but that, like Elverata, was forgotten. I shall never see her again! she a good, honest, and religious girl; though nothing here below, in heaven she will be more than a *femme de chambre*. Some may well say,

> "Happy those who linger yet
> The steep ascent to climb,
> For jewels lie like treasures set
> Upon the breast of Time."

COUP D'ETAT OF NAPOLEON III.

ON the morning of the 3d and 4th of Dec.. the fate of Paris, like a stormy sea, was rocking to and fro in the minds of this versatile and fickle people.

On the 2d of December, the morning after the ascent of the members of the National Assembly, I went to the Boulevards to see how the populace took this daring of the Presidents. The place was crowded with groups discussing the importance of this blow to their liberties. Old, white-headed men were making speeches in different places within sight. But while they were making speeches Louis Napoleon was at the Palace decreeing laws for this particular occasion, and he was not only in the Palace quelling the populace, but the very same day he rode through the Boulevards at the head of soldiers, and people shouted *vive l' empereur*. How and why they said this, when as yet they had none, remains to be seen. That night fifty or sixty thousand soldiers slept in the streets of Paris, and cavalry stood close to the side walk for miles without one single

---

the fate of Paris . . . : See note to p. 35.

break of ranks. The soldiers had their rations carried to
them. Next morning, the 3d, the rebels commenced their
work of destruction in spite of the soldiers. The news
came into Paris from all parts of France that a hundred
thousand soldiers were rapidly marching to the assistance
of the army and sustanance of the republic. But this did
not intimidate the factions, The soldiers though now one
hundred thousand strong, right in the city, they had to
keep on the march, up, one street and down another, to
keep down the barricade builders. I saw a strong wall
built across a street in a quarter of an hour. They go
about peaceable in droves until they pass the soldiers and
then with pickaxes and crowbars and all manner of iron
implements dig up the flag-stones, door-sills and stone
steps, and place them one upon another until they get them
head high. They leave small apertures to poke their pistols
and guns through, and therefrom they fight the soldiers
who cannot, except by accident, shoot through the apertures. If the soldiers come down behind them to hem them
in, they jump over the barricade and they are as well there
as on the other side. But the soldiers are in a critical
condition fighting barricaders, because they have their
friends on the top of the houses and in each story, throwing down all manner of heavy things, such as pots, skillets,
pans, chairs, beds, plates, dishes, tumblers and bottles on
the heads of the soldiers until they are intimidated enough
to stand from under. I saw one old orator leading the

rebels up by the side of the soldiers and trying to persuade some of them to say they would not fire on the citizens if they were ordered. The captain of these troops told him if he did not leave off talking with the soldiers that he would have him shot. He would not, and was placed back against the wall and shot through.

On the 4th, precisely at two o'clock, the firing of muskets and cannon were heard from all parts of the city of Paris. The cannon balls ran through whole blocks of buildings, but the destruction was not, as one might suppose, bustling but made clear, rounded holes of its own size, and passed on so rapid it left no bustling confusion. Where it touched, it done its work. When the firing commenced I was in the crowd on the *Boulevard des Italian* with the crowd that was being shot at. Some fell, and I, with hundreds, ran over them. I fell, and a dozen or so leaped over me. Like a tangled rabbit I rose and went faster than ever. I ran down the *rue Lafitte,* trying to get into some of those large palace doorways, but all was firmly barred. Having run clear past my own house, No. 43, *rue Lafitte,* I only discovered my mistake by observing a squad of soldiers behind *l'eglise l'orette,* loading and firing over some dead bodies that had already fallen beneath their fire. Like a rabbit again, I took the back track, and my good old porter saw me from the third story, and descended and opened one foot of his *porte firme,* and said with a cheek flushed with fear, " *Entree vite.*" I was about to

---

Like a tangled rabbit: The rabbit, the trickster figure in the Brer Rabbit tales, stands for the African-American. In using this figure to describe himself, Dorr is identifying with the African-American oral tradition.
l'eglise l'orette: A church in Paris called Notre Dame de Lorette.
porte firme: The correct French would be *porte firmée,* which means "closed door."
"Entree vite": Come in quickly. The correct written form would be *Entrez vite.* Here, as elsewhere, Dorr uses a phonetic form of the expression.

kiss the old man, but he was not inclined to enjoy such a luxury, most especially as I had failed to take the advice he gave me the morning before, "*pas allez dans la rue.*"

About an hour after this the streets of Paris were as empty as a ball room after the festal scene. It is a wonderful sight to see the streets of Paris void of its moving mass of humanity. Like the streets of Pompeii, it reminds one of the victory of destruction. Paris looked as if it was mourning for those thousands that were fleetly moving on to eternity. Next day hundreds of ladies and gentlemen who were innocently killed, lay under a shed in Paris, to be recognized by their friends, and buried. You could not get close to them, not closer than ten feet, and then look along through the glass that kept you and the scent in your own places. There lay some of the gayest of Paris, with their fine kids on as they had fallen ; their watches and diamonds denoted their bearing, while their countenances said in their expression, "in the midst of life we are in death."

There can be no mistake but that these were people that were trying to get ont of danger, but were overtaken ere they reached the barrier of safety.

The poor horses in the streets of Paris looked round on the crowded and thronged streets with considerable amazement at man's convulsions. People, horses, birds, shops, and even the weather resembled the picture of discontent. The graceful hanging trees of the Champs Elysees, and

---

"*pas allez dans la rue*": Don't go in the street. The correct expression would be *ne pas allez dans la rue*, but the *ne* is often omitted in colloquial speech. This kind of usage suggests that Dorr had more than a textbook familiarity with French and that he was, indeed, raised in New Orleans.

Tuilleries, are disturbed by the bayonet, as the soldiers stand under them, for a sort of shield from the drizzling weather, while they keep the populace back from the National Assembly. The night after this awful contention of the people against the army, was as still and lonesome a one as ever the gay spirit of France was awed with. This night was as interesting to Frenchmen, as the 20th of January, 1793, the night before the execution of Louis the sixteenth, and which history describes thus: "Paris was, by the direction of the government, illuminated on the night of the 20th, and no person was permitted to go at large in the streets. Strong bodies of armed troops patroled in every district of that immense metropolis, the sounds of carriages ceased, the streets appeared deserted, except by the patrols, and the whole city was buried in an awful silence. About two o'clock on the morning of the fatal 21st, voices were heard, throughout the gloom, of lamentation and distress, but whence they came, or what they were, no one has ever discovered. On Monday morning, as the clock struck 8, he was summoned to his fate. He was conducted to a coach belonging to the Mayor of Paris, in which were two soldiers of the *gendarmerie*; the most profound silence prevailed while the carriage advanced slowly to the scaffold; Louis mounted the platform with a firm step and unaltered countenace, and was preparing to address them, when the ruffian *Sauterre*, who commanded the guard, cried out, no speeches, no speeches, and suddenly the drums beat

---

20th of January, 1793: Here, as elsewhere, Dorr is correct about historical facts.
gendarmerie: French state police.

and the trumpets sounded. The unfortunate monarch, then, with apparent serenity, placed his head upon the block, the axe fell, and in an instant he ceased to live in this world. So perished Louis the XVI, a prince whose heart nature had formed of the best materials, and who, from the first accession to power, appeared to make his first object, his peoples' happiness. He was an excellent husband and a good father."

Though the laws on both occasions were executed with great faith and promptness, they were by no means pacific to the nation. There is still too much royal blood in France to allow the seed of republicanism to prosper spontaneously heedless of their interests. Though they readily admit that Louis the fifteenth was a better sultan than a king of France, and that Louis Phillippe dissipated the throne by being an illegitimate heir, still they cannot look upon that as sufficient reason to rid them of their vested ancestral rights.

The French are full of that ambition that came from Orleans in female attire, to give back to royalty some hope of yet governing a versatile people. But if Louis Napoleon, the President of France, wants to rise higher, he must consult the legitimists of France, or he will never find bone and sinew for his cruel *coup de etat.*

THE SECRETS OF A PARIS LIFE, AND WHO KNOWS THEM.

READER, can a man dream with his eyes open? or can a man see with them shut? Before you say no, bear in mind that man is the shadow of his maker; and life, a dream. As to the latter part of the query, the answer may be emphatically no! Then let me dream of what I saw.

One night my faculties fell asleep upon all the world's eider down, but these things, my faculties, could not sleep on, I saw myself going along by the quietest looking, but gayest palace of every day resort of noblemen and monied men, that decorates the Boulevard. It is not the magic No. from the corner of the *Rue la Fitte.* On the first floor is all the pleasure a monied man could momentarily crave; but the second floor looked gayer, and the third gayer still. I could see ladies and gentlemen coming in groups of two, four, and six, every quarter of a minute.

It was six o'clock, as near as I can recollect the dream. They commenced sitting down at different tables, while some were hanging up hats, and others looking around

---

Reader, can a man dream . . . : This is a central chapter illustrating Dorr's intent not simply to report what he saw but to use the genre of travel writing to fashion an empowering selfhood.

as if they were hunting something like what other
people had; some of the tables were larger than others;
according to their number was the measure thereof.   The
gentlemen looked as dignified as giraffes, whilst the ladies
looked the picture of birds of Paradise more especially
where fine feathers contributed.   Some were placing their
chairs in as agreeable a position as their inward idea could
allow them to do with propriety.   Towards the end of this
Palace, in the direction of the Boulevards, now sprang up a
volley of small, or not very loud, musket-like reports, but
as nobody was afraid, no harm could be done.   Then I
could see the waiters pouring into some glasses like Dutch
churns, upside down, some hot, smoking stuff that boiled
over; it was so hot, that a man might well fear for the ladies
mouths being burnt when they took hold of it as if they
did not see it, but merely wished to comply with the desire
of their beaux.   I expected every moment to hear them
scream, but they were not afraid of it.   The waiters were
running to and fro with bottles of all colors.   Here one
turned up some smaller glasses and poured in something
like blood.   If it was blood it was pure as Abel's sacrafice;
I never before saw redder from veins.   The next occupation of the waiter, was bringing different kinds of soups.
I looked on the *carte* and saw a dozen different kinds; some
I never read of before.   I looked out of the window on
the *Rue la Fitte*, and saw as many as twenty carriages stand-

ing before one another, and from them descending ladies and gentlemen in pairs, running up stairs with perfect gusto.

It is six o'clock as I have said, and I will leave those scenes and tell what more I dreamt, but will return again. I thought I pushed my way through crowds of people, and moved along the Boulevards about four squares, until I came to an extraordinary fine and fashionable street called Vivienne, and I followed it about two squares until my attention was attracted by an immense stone building, taking up one whole square. It looked like the temples I had read of, and I asked a man what it meant, who said it is a place where all the rich people go every day at 1 o'clock to make money, and some loose; they call it " Bourse." He assured me that its financiering had made "countless thousands mourn." I next walked into a Caffee filled with ladies and gentlemen and found a seat. A few minutes afterwards a ballet girl entered and seated herself for *la creme.* I then called for some cream and we eat on the same side of the same table. I asked her if it was good? she said she liked it, and asked me if mine was the same. As the color was different I could not say, without tasting hers, and we put our glasses together and satisfied ourselves on the difference, after which we took a *vere du vin* at the expense of one of us.

It is now 11 o'clock, and I said I would return to the

---

vere du vin: Glass of wine. The correct French would be *verre de vin.*

" Maison Doree." Having reached this all-hour sought place, I saw the very same people I saw seat themselves at 6 o'clock. They were somewhat changed in color; they all looked rosier and better enabled to take hold of anything they had to do. The gentlemen looked more sociable, and the ladies—I won't say more bold, but less timid. When a gentleman had anything to communicate, he was not obliged to exert himself in reaching, because the ladies would meet him half way. Everything was so harmonious that one could not go through the laborious task of telling his wish, without assistance from his hearer. Every few minutes something like a rallying remnant of a weak soldier's gun would go off, and the glasses would smoke as though each one was a volcano. Every minute or two a couple would rise, and before the gentleman could give his arm the lady would reach for it. Even their tempers seemed to fit, as the ocean does the earth, all around and through. Whilst I was thus dreaming, the pillow became insufferable, and I must say it awoke me. I thought I looked out of the window on the moving surface of the Seine. The moon was shining down on its ripples with a most admirable light of solemn grandeur. Stillness reigned such as I had never seen in Paris, and all the time I stood gazing upon that famous stream, not once did that queer dream enter my mind. I jumped into bed and soon fell asleep, and soon got into the old habit, so I dreamt. How

---

"Maison Doree": Gilded House.

particular a man ought to be, when about to do anything for the first time, for, let it be good or bad, the mind will be tempered with the same sterile or fertile nature, as that of the preceding act. I thought I was again at the agreeable Maison Doree, and I looked upon the walled clock, and the hour hand stood at 2. The hall below stairs was as empty as the marble hall, where the true lover dreamed he dwelt among vassals and serfs. But I also dreamed, *which pleased me most,* that I saw very many beautiful women walking up and down the sidewalk with an apparent air of hunting for something; not that they had lost anything they ever possessed, but something to be found. I thought one came up to me with her dress fully two feet shorter in front than behind, I mean to say it looked so from what I could see, and said to me *"quelle heure it el?"* I told her 2 o'clock; she then looked puzzled, as if she was sure I did not know what she meant by speaking to me at that late hour. Then she started one way and turned and went the other. As she passed me she gave her dress a jerk in front that raised it so high that I almost saw the whole of a pair of the whitest stockings I had seen since I left the Dutch, who don't wear stockings at all. My curiosity was that of children on a Christmas morning, and I started after her in the same earnestnesss to see if there was anything good inside the stockings. I found that the supposed stocking, like Santa Claus, was all imagination. Thus ends the dream witth open eyes.

"quelle heure it el?": What time is it? The correct expression would be *quelle heure est-il?* but the one Dorr uses is a patois French.

Said the fast Countess of Blessington, "Oh commend me
to the comforts of a French bed ; its soft and even mattress,
its light curtains, and genial *couvre pied* of eider down;
commend me, also, to a French *cuisine*, with its soup *sans*
pepper, its cutlet *a la minute,* and its *poulet au jus,* its *cafe
a la creme,* and its desserts. But defend me from its slam-
ming of French doors, and the shaking of French windows,
&c." I like not the noise like the one in Paris; it is an
amalgamated one, such as never was heard in another city on
earth. The noise of Paris is a variegated one, like humming
of bees, or a serpent's hiss when they cannot be seen. Sometimes its cabs alone, at another carts filled with groups of
theatre actors, from the *Opera Comique, Theatre Francois,
Ambique, Grand Opera, or Hippodrome.* Or if it is early in
the morning, it is sure to be some gay crowds returning
from some wild and exciting amusement, such as only
French can enjoy without remorse. When you hear a
noise in Paris, you can no more tell its cause, than you can
tell the composition of a fricassee. It may be a good rabbit,
or a better cat, the skin of the former lying on the table to
prove its identity, When you see woodcocks in the window
of a second rate *restaurateur,* you must not be sure that the
cook is putting his herbs among the joints of the woodcock
you have ordered, instead of a diseased owl that was caught
in the barn, for French cooks are not to be scared by an owl.
The more he can dress a rat like a squirrel, the greater his

Countess of Blessington: Marguerite, countess of Blessington (1789–
1849), published *A Journal of Conversations with Lord Byron* and
The Idler in France.
couvre pied: Coverlet or bedspread.
a la minute: Minute steak.
poulet au jus: Chicken with gravy.

celebrity as an epicure of the most refined taste. If you go to market in Paris, you will see under a butcher's stall, whole herds of rabbits, for rabbits are domestic animals in France. This butcher lives at the upper end of the market, and has nothing to do with *Mons. Ledeau,* who lives at the other end, and who sells little cats under the disguise of amusing *les enfants de Paris.* But *Mons. Feteau,* the restaurateur, knows both, and takes particular care to invite *Mons. Ledeau chez Lui* to take dinner with him, when they have a good deal of unknown talk. After this interview, the trade in rabbits gets dull, and the vender wonders who can sell them on more advantageous terms than he can. He looks all around the market, and finds that his price is the usual price. It never enters his head that cats are substituted for rabbits.

Now reader, don't accuse me of trying to become conspicuous by asserting more than others, for you know nothing about it, and I do. I have seen a landlord stand behind a post in his own restaurant, watching some of his patrons trying to cut what he called *poulet* (chicken), but no mortal man could tell what it was but a French *cuisineur.* I have dined at the *Maison Doree, Trois Freres, Cafe Anglaise,* and *Vachettes.* and then gradually down to the lowest grade, the socialists, and I ought to know something about it.

Oh, how delightful it is to walk on the Champ Elysee

and take a seat among the French girls, *au fait*, and order your *caffee au lait*. Then take from your pocket a *sou*, sit cross legged and toss it up and down, and turn it over and, look at it, and while waiting for the light guitar, to fend off those nimble fingers, that are taking from it its sweetest notes, you can think what an immense deal of pleasure you are getting for the mere anticipation of a *sou*. Then look around, not slyly, but boldly, and you see some unassuming French *demoiselle* gazing upon you with such riveted force of interest, that the lashes of her eye moveth not. After this you walk into some *valentino cassino, or jardin,* and you will see some 80 or 100 modes of cupids and Psyches, keeping time to a Parisian band, and there will appear to your mind a perfect agreeing correspondence between the music and the figures that dance around it. Never will you see the right foot of one couple up while the left foot of another is down, such perfection of dancing is to be found in all classes in Paris.

Very candid, frank and free is a Frenchmen. If one admires a lady, she knows it almost before an opportunity presents itself. If he is encouraging a useless desire, he always manages it before it can do a serious injury. Little trouble dwells within the mind of a Frenchman; he makes much of to-day, to-morrow's trouble must dawn or die with itself. He finds more pleasure in going

---

au fait: In fact.
demoiselle: Young lady.

to the opera, with his five francs, than he does by sitting in the house, waiting for the morrow that never comes, or if it does come, bringing with it a greater anxiety and love for another morrow.

There is an amusement in Paris, which language is inadequate to express the vulgarity of. It is called the *"industrious fleas."* The name does not indicate the performance. It changes its location every night in fear of the police. Its supporters are merely curious young men, who wish to see as strange a sight as the mind of woman can picture. Their performance commences with a dozen beautiful women habited like Eve before she devised the fig leaf covering. They first appear in the form of a wreath, with each one's head between another's legs; the rest must be imagined. *Au revoir.*

ROME AND ST. PETER'S CHURCH.

By the gate on the southern side, on the 28th of March, 1852, I entered the "Holy City," just as day was turning to night. I moved slowly along by the venerable walls of the great St. Peter's church, in a shackling old *viturino*. A celebrated writer says it is built on the site of the palace of Julius Cæsar. He also says the extent of ground covered by the ruined and inhabited parts of Rome amounts to four and twenty miles. You there find eighty halls of the eighty eminent kings; from king Targuin, to king Pepin, the father of Charlemange, who first conquered Spain, and wrested it from the Mahomedans. In the outskirts of Rome, he said, there is the palace of Titus, who was rejected by the 300 senators, in consequence of having wasted three years in the conquest of Jerusalem, which, according to their will, he ought to have accomplished in two years. There is likewise the hall of Vespasian, a very large and strong building, also the hall of king Galba,

---

viturino: A small horse-drawn carriage. The correct spelling would be *vetturino,* meaning small vehicle.

Titus: Roman emperor, 79–81 A.D.

Vespasian: Roman emperor (9–79 A.D.), founder of the Flavian dynasty, which marked the shift from a narrow Roman to an imperial Roman Empire.

containing 360 windows, the circumference of this palace
is nearly three miles, and on this very three miles of earth,
a battle was fought in times of yore, and more than one
hundred thousand fell, whose bones are hung up there
even to the present day. Now Rome is the leader of all
Christendom, and St. Peters' yearly carnivals are the glory
of Rome, instead of the gladiatorial festivals in the Colisseum.
Some writers assert that it is only the forum upon the site
of the palace of the Cæsars. Cooper says in his excursions
in Italy, that the first palace of Nero must have occupied
the whole of the Palatine hill, with perhaps the exception of
a temple or two. The ground round the Colisseum, and
all the land as far as the Esquiline, and even to the verge
of the the Quirinal, a distance exceeding a mile; this was
occupying, moreover, the heart of the town, although a
portion of the space was occupied by gardens, and other
embellishments. When this building was burned, he
returned to the Palatine, repaired the residence of Augustus,
and rebuilt his residence with so much magnificence, that
the new palace was called the "golden house;" this
building also extended to the Esquiline, though it was
never finished. Vespasian and Titus, more moderate than
the descendants of the Cæsars, demolished all the new
parts of the palace, and caused the Colisseum and the baths
that bear the name of the latter, to be constructed on the
spot; the emperors were all elected, and they found it

Cooper: Dorr is probably referring to James Fenimore Cooper's
Gleanings in Europe, Italy (1838).

necessary to consnlt the public taste and good.   Thus we
find the remains of two of the largest structures of the
world, now standing within the ground once occupied by
the palace of the Cæsars, on which they appear as little
more than points.   From this time, the emperors confined
themselves to the palatine, the glory of which gradually
departed.   It is said that the palace, as it was subsequently
reduced, remained standing in a great measure, as recently
as the 8th century, and that it was even inhabited in the
7th, so says Cooper.

Having been anxious to see the Pope of Rome, Pius IX, I
was a frequent visitor of the Carnival, and at last got a
good look at the great man.   He was seated on a divan,
which rested on the shoulders of twelve cardinals, or
senators of Rome; he was crowned with a gorgeously
jewelled crown, as the eye of man need wish to gaze on.
Ten thousand people were in the church at the time, and
they would carry the Pope from one aisle to another.
The people all would fall on their knees, and the great
man would bless them in the name of God, and the organ
would peal its bassy notes of Te Deum, from east to west,
and north to south, whilst the alarum from the belfry
jarred my heart strings.

Rome, said a great traveler, is well known; authors of
veracity assure us that for seven hundred years, she was
mistress of the world, but although their writings should

not affirm this, would there not be sufficient evidence in all
the grand edifices now existing, in those columns of marble,
those statues. Add to the quantity of relics that are there,
so many things that our Lord has touched with his own
fleshy fingers, such numbers of holy bodies of Apostles,
Martyrs, Confessors, and Virgins; in short, so many
churches, where the Holy Pontiffs, have granted full Indul-
gences for sin.

This writer that spoke of these true merits of the city
of Rome, was among these great and magnificient ruins
of Rome, in the 14th century. His name was Bertrand de
la Bracquiere, a Lord of Vieux Chateau, counseller and
first Esquire carver, to Phillip, Duke of Burgundy, living
at that age in Ghent.

One day when it was very warm, I went down to the
Tiber to waste a little time reflectively, where the golden
candlestick that was brought from Jerusalem fell off the
bridge and never was afterwards found. Whilst I laid there
on its banks, listening to its most inaudible murmur a Jew
came and stretched himself close to my feet. I asked him
if he recollected who it was that Plutarch says was con-
demned to the hideons punishment of being nailed up in a
barrel with serpents and thrown in the Tiber to float on to
the sea? He had never heard of such a thing. I then
asked him if he was aware that the golden candlestick out
of the temple of Solomon lay at the bottom of that muddy

stream ? he said yes, and added that the Pope had been
offered millions of piastres by the Jews to let them turn
the current of the Tiber twenty miles above Rome, that they
might recover all the lost and hidden treasure of nearly
three thousand years' standing, but the Pope had refused
because he was too superstitious to allow the Tiber's current to be changed.

My attention was just at this time drawn to a large old
building that had the bearing of royalty deeply marked on
its furrowed decay. I asked its use, and was informed that
it was a maccaroni manufactory. I drew nigh, and stood,
in company with dozens of girls, looking through its de-
cayed apertures. I saw hnndreds of men walking about in
a perfect state of nudity, and also as many more moving
round at quicker step. I would discover every few moments
a couple of these that seemed to be mantled with small
reeds of a bending nature, step on a platform and commence
turning round, like crazy men imitating the spinning of a
top, but I could discover nothing of their intention until
they walked off the platform, when I could plainly see that
they had divested themselves of something I knew not what.

The way they make maccaroni in Rome, is thus: when it
is hot or warm, the men stand by the aperture that squeezes
it into a reed-like shape, and wind it round their bodies
until they are totally covered or mantled, and then they
walk in great haste in a circle until it is nearly cool, after

which they walk on the aforesaid platform and unwind themselves from its cooling grasp, and there it stays until it becomes totally dry, after which they box it for export. That which is made for home consumption is not made on so extensive a scale, and different ideas of neatness is needed lest it affect the home consumption.

Three days it took me to pass through the "Vatican." It is the great gallery of fine arts, and the Pope lives in one part of this Palace. The Carnival being over, I took one day to go to Tivoli to see an old temple and olive orchard and the vast ruins of the emperor Adrian's brick palace, after which I returned to Rome, and bought some mosaic work in breast pin jewelry, hired a viturino and four, went to St. Peters and took a last farewell glance at St. Peter, who stands in his statue dignity over an altar with his keys of Heaven, and left Rome in its decay of tyrannical monuments for Naples, its bay and Vesuvius.

NAPLES AND ITS CRAFT.

AFTER twenty days sight-seeing in Rome, observe me seated in the front of a viturino on my way to Naples. E. G. Squires, the author of a book of discoveries, is seated in one of the back seats. He is a little man full of humor, and a man to judge him by his looks and manners would have a hard task to steer from error. He is well versed in Roman lore. We were now an hour and half out from Rome, and he said "look there ahead, those old walls we are going under is the walls of old Rome, and that high archway, with those splendid pillars of carved stone, is the gate leading into Rome via the Appian road from Naples." We passed through these walls and Rome was forgotton, in the matters of interest to which he directed our attention. As we came up to the pretty little ruined city Albano, he said, "there, gentlemen, is the tomb of Pompey the Great." It was a tall monumental tomb of white marble, but fallen on all sides by the wreck of the weather. We entered Albano and dined, and paid a visit to the Veil of Diana, whose

---

viturino: See note to p. 96.

E. G. Squires, the author of a book of discoveries: Dorr might be referring to Ephraim George Squier, an American archaeologist who explored the antiquities of the Mississippi Valley and wrote works on Central America.

temple was here at Albano. This city occupies the site of the palace of Pompey the Great and Domitian. The Veil of Diana is a lake of a few hundred yards round, and hemmed in on all sides by cliffs of fertility. Two days and a half brought me to the back part of the city of Naples. In coming to Naples by this route you are some hours going down hill, but as the lombard poplar trees are so numerous, it is impossible to get a look at Naples; occasionally I could hear the roar of Vesuvius and the hum of business, coming by the force of the breeze from the bay on the other side. All at once I came out on an open descending slope, but, a quarter of a mile ahead, the lombardy poplars intercepted our view, still over their tops, off to the left of Naples, I could see Vesuvius like a sleeping giant with his flag of wrath ascending on high. The flag of smoke was as still as a standing cloud, and it stood like God on the earth, but spreading above in the Heavens.

Napoli is the city's name, and its meaning is New City, and we call it Naples.

I don't think that one contented man can be found in the whole city of Naples, with its 450,000 souls. Every time this growling, burning mountain roars it jars the whole city; organ grinders give themselves as little trouble about Vesuvius as any other class, and the streets are full of them. They stand all day playing away in the streets as if they had no where to run to, whilst all house tenants, citizens, king and priests, run in the streets for fear Vesuvius will spit fire and brimstone on them, for she has once or twice proved that she, like God, had no respect of persons. Naples is at least five miles off, but they looked to me as if they were only a quarter of a mile apart. It is believed by philosophical men that Vesuvius has burnt out her bowels for miles under the shallow bay, and also under Naples.

I went to Pompeii and Herculanium, two great cities that Vesuvius, in her tipsy spree, belched all over, destroying population, temples, theatres, and gladiatorial arenas. Expeditions from different parts of the world were here, excavating crowns of diamonds ; and hundreds of thousands of scnddies worth of the rarest jemmed jewelry has been found, even upon the parched bones of notorious victims to this hideous spree.

Naples was founded one thousand and three hundred years before the Christian era, and still escapes this awful calamity. Generation after generation has lived and died in this fear, and still Naples is yet the most wicked city on the face of the globe. It shows that hell-fire preaching will never advance man in this world, or better prepare him for another. Nothing but an educated mind can ever understand the mission of christianity. If tyranny can ever do anything with the mind of man, it had full scope here. The Neapolitans, reared under such fearful influences of wrath, must naturally be tempered with surrounding influences. To see a club slain man in Naples is no object of pity; their mind is forever placed on wholesale calamities, and nothing short of that can excite sympathy in such a people. They can fight well because they are always well prepared to fight, or be annihilated. When the great Carthagenian, who was so victorious over the Romans, at the well known battle of Thrasimene, came here to take Naples, he was so much frightened at the walls, that he would not undertake to beseige the city. Cumae was the first name of this city, but its inhabitants being a very jealous people, fell out, and destroyed it; but it was soon rebuilt, and then it was renamed New City, Napoli, when its walls obtained the strength that scared the son of Hamilcar, who had come away from Carthage, leaving behind him a people who could never believe that the Italians could be whipped, not even by Hannibal, until he sent three bushels of gold rings back, that was taken from the fingers of conquered Italians, to prove it.

There is three hundred churches in Naples, but the vestry of priesthood is no sign of the true temple of wisdom. The lower classes are craft ridden from the faggest end of an intelligent class, to the uttermost peak of sublime ignorance. The moral authority has great power over those who profess to be the followers of the Church; even the king himself, is afraid of the priest. In illustration of this I must relate an anecdote on the present king of Naples,

---

present king of Naples . . . king of the two Sicilies: King Ferdinand II.

whose title is better known as the king of the two Sicilies.
A good, and honest intentioned priest one day called on
the king to obtain a certain small sum of money from his
honor, as a starting point of collection to build a church at
a certain place.   The king, who loves money much, refused
to start the ball rolling by contributing the first subscription.
The good father, somewhat astonished, stood sometime,
thinking over the chances of getting anything after the
king's refusal, put his hand under his ground colored
gown to lay hold of his handkerchief to wipe his nose and
eyes of their weeping.   The king took fright, and ran to
the bell and rang furiously, the guard came running in and
arrested the priest, but to their great pleasure they discovered
that the king was frightened at the priest's motion for his
handkerchief, instead of a stilleto.   The people got wind of
it, and laughed at the scary old king so that he dare not go
out.

   This, old ugly king has been trying to make some improvements in the way of morality.   He has appropriated
a small portion of the city to the safe keeping of lewd women.   It is about three squares of this city being walled in,
and all women found and proven in adultery are to be con-
demned to the inside of these walls until the city authorities
become satisfied that they are sufficiently punished.   Police
are stationed at the gate and no one but spectators are
allowed to go in and out, except an old woman who acts as

their steward. All foreigners are allowed to go in once, but I don't suppose foreigners ever wished to go in more than once. When I was in, the Lazaroni asked me if I would allow him to spend a quarter of my bag of change to see the women perform. I, not knowing what he meant, said "Yes." He gave a 25c. piece to one woman, and there was a hundred in that group, and said something in Italian, when, as many as wished to claim stock in the 25 cents commenced showing their nakedness, to the horror of man's sensual curiosity. I saw fifty women show what I had never legally seen before. I must end this chapter and commence another of more superstition, of St. Janarius and his Blood.

ST. JANARIUS AND HIS BLOOD.

In the centre of Naples, on a very high hill, is a splendid old castle or fort. Myself and two American ladies winded round its base upwards, till we reached its gates. Our guide beat there some time before its old lord would hear; we handed him our permit from below to enter ,and he said "walk in," in the French tongue. These two American ladies and their father seemed to make quite an agreeable impression on the commander of the castle or fort. He invited us into his parlor where he asked us many disguised questions, such as; "how do you like Naples?" "when are you going to leave and what directions will you take from here?" was some of his questions. Having "pumped" us as dry as he could, he called a guard and put us under escort to see the wonders of this old tyrant mound. Cannons were pointed from the loopholes of this fort to all parts of the city. The people are afraid to rebel against the laws of Ferdinand II, because orders from the palace to this castle can come under ground. The king has a private path miles under ground to get to this castle when besieged

in his palace. It is said that this fort can destroy the city
in a few hours; can batter it all down and set it on fire
with its shells, and burn it up, and as the property belongs
to the citizens they keep quiet. The old man now invited
us back to his saloon and asked us our opinions of this, his
castle; of course it was all we anticipated and more too.
Whilst he was delighted with the ladies' answers to his
questions, I walked out in the court, and the lazaroni or
guide called my attention to the open register, where all
visitors' names are recorded, and glanced at the following
record of that morning: " *Mons. Millenberger et deau dame;
Compte Fello de Amerique et une jeune homme.*" This was
indeed laughable, but to make it more absurd, my old guide
informed me that he was aware of our nobility some days
ago. I inquired of him how it was possible for him to find
out such a mystery. He smiled very knowingly and assured me that he was possessed of peculiar tact for finding out
such things. Then in his confirmation of his skill in fath-
oming this hidden secret, he told me of a Mr. Rice, a powerful lord of South Carolina, who would be an heir to an
immense estate if he lived long enough, and of his noble
bearing, and how Mr. R. tried to conceal it from him, but
it couldn't be done, and which Mr. Rice had to acknowledge.
Then he went on to show me why Americans ought not to
try and conceal such things as they eventually lost the best
accomodation the hotels could afford, by not letting it be
known who it was wanted them. He also suggested that

"*Mons. Millenberger et deau dame; Compte Fello de Amerique et une
jeune homme*": Dorr often makes the pretensions of Americans the
butt of his humor, much in the manner of Mark Twain in *Innocents
Abroad.*

American noblemen ought to wear some peculiar mark or sign that they may be distinguished from those of an inferior dignity. I for once felt like driving the good-natured old fool away, but as he was so bigoted with his own errors I told him that all noblemen of American peculiarities did have signs about them unmistakeable. Here his curiosity rose to such a pitch he asked me to make it known to him so that he might hereafter know how to treat such worth. I told him that if ever he came across an American of Arkansas or Texas, to get behind him when seated and look over his left shoulder, in his bosom, and he will most likely see something like an elephant's tusk, but it was nothing more nor less than what was called a toothpick, and when he saw that, it would be to his advantage to be mighty polite. The old man believes now he has the insignia of an American prince, and intends treating him with due respect to his high position.

From this Fort I took a ride to Baie, and after two hours' ride I reached it. Two thousand years ago it was a great city where Cæsar and Cicero dwelt a great part of their time. The site of their palaces are yet discernable. The hot baths out of the earth are here yet, and I took one. No doubt but they are heated, running under the bay from Vesuvius on the other side. A few hundred yards out in the bay is the smallest island I ever saw to have a town of thousands of souls on it. It is about a mile in circumference. The town takes up almost all of the island of Procida. The inhabitants are nearly all Greek descendants, and are celebrated for keeping up the Greek fashions. The old guide insisted on us going into the heart of Procida, where he would show us the curious costumes. Having waited in an old dirty room some time for the scene, a rough working girl came into the room and stood some time. The old man asked me how I liked it? but I could'nt see anything different from other women about the town He told her to turn around, when he called my attention to some plaiting around the waist of the woman's dress. She now whispered something to our guide, which, when translated, meant that she had her soap to make, and would like to discontinue the performance as the show was out. He said we must give her a couple of pauls for her trouble of dressing and un-dressing. This old man kept us laughing all the way back to Naples. When leaving Baie, passing some old magnifi-cent ruins, he said, "Gentlemen, that is the ruins of the palace of Lucullus, the greatest eater that ever was in Italy." Then he commenced relating Plutarch's history of Lucullus' style of living. He told us of the single dish that was expensive to the tune of 1,200 francs. Here the old man licked out his tongue, in token of his approbation of its being good. This old man has a country seat and town residence. He showed us, on our way out, his country seat; it consists of an old brick building, that in times of yore must have been used by somebody, who had a house, as a stable, and being an enterprising man, his mouth watered for it as a filthy retreat from Naples, when he can get no labor, such as he is now occupied with. We give him about forty cents a day, and he finds himself.

In Napoli is a church of fearful renown. It is built upon the site of the temple of Apollo; it was commenced by Charles the first, and finished by Charles the second, in the twelfth century. It is built of stone, and pillars of stone, from all parts of Africa, brought here in conquest. In it is buried the aforesaid Charles. This is the church of St. Janarius; a large statue of St. Janarius is represented seated, and always ready to bless the people. In a small tabernacle, with silver doors, is preserved the head and two vials of the Saint's blood, said to have been collected by a Neapolitan lady during his martyrdom. This blood becomes miraculously liquid, whenever it is placed before the head of St. Janarius. The ceremony of this miracle is repeated three times a year, that is, during eight days in the month of May, eight days during the month of September, and on the day of protection, on the 16th of December. This miracle is to the Neapolitans a constant object of devotion and astonishment, of which no one that has not been present, can form a just idea. When the liquifaction of the blood takes place immediately, the joy of the people knows no bounds; but if the operation of the miracle is retarded one moment, the cries and groaning of the people rend the air; for at Naples the procrastination of this miracle is considered the prestage of some great misfortune;

In Napoli is a church of fearful renown. . . . in the twelfth century: There are obviously some factual errors in the text. Charles I was king of Sicily from 1266 to 1285; Charles II was king of peninsular Sicily from 1285 to 1309.

the grief, particularly of the women, is so great, that the blood never fails to become liquid, and resume its consistency, on each of the eight days; so that every one may see and kiss the blood of St. Janarius, in as liquid a state as when it first issued from his veins. The city of Naples has been in danger of being destroyed by the eruption of Mt. Vesuvius, by earthquakes, and other calamities, such as war, pestilence, &c., &c., but it has always been delivered by the blood of this mighty Saint. A lady writer says: "At one time the blood was rather slow about doing its duty, when their hypocritical priest says to the people, that the blood would never liquidate so long as they allowed the French to keep possession of the town. As soon as the French general heard this, he sent notice to the people that if the priest did not make the blood liquidate in ten minutes, off went his head. There was great lamentation for the priest, and the whole city was sympathizing with him, as his time was short; but at the expiration of nine minutes and three quarters the blood liquidated,

CONSTANTINOPLE.

ON the second day of May I glided out on the beautiful bay of Naples, and steered towards the east, where the wise men lived, and the light rose up. The first piece of terra firma next discovered was Etna, in Sicily. Sicily, before the crusade of king Siguard, was governed by Dukes and Earls. Mussinna is the only town of any particular note, on this fertile island. Mt. Etna, while at Musina, hides half of the firmament from your view, but when seen at eventide from the deck of a receding vessel, it seems to have sunk in a mole hole. It takes two days carriage ride around its base, to reach its top. Six days out from Naples brought our good vessel to Syria, a city in Greece, with 14,000 inhabitants. It is a charming sight to look at from your vessel, on account of its resemblance to *wall hung pigeon houses*. From the sea, you look at a mountain, with hundreds of systematical white spots clinging to its sides, and which proves to be Syria.

The ship stopped here a day, and all the passengers, and

the rest of mankind, went ashore. The men were quite handsome for such a rough country; four or five young men and myself, were determined to see some of the Syrian ladies, if possible. On we went to the top of the city, through very narrow streets, and few ran over fifty yards without ending, and taking some unknown direction. After great exertion we reached the highest house, but, like Moses from his Pisgah, we saw the land but not its fruits. We were still inclined to prosecute our search, until our minds came to some definite conclusion. An exclamation of joy burst forth from one of our company, indicating success. We all moved closer to our guide, who, most wonderful to behold, had discovered the figure of a woman with her back towards us. We passed respectfully by her, trying to conceal our emotion of success. The first that passed her, quickly turned round as if he would speak to our companions, just as you have seen a young lady walk a little ahead of her companion, to have an excuse to look back at some young gent who seemed to have admired her when passing, and lo! this woman's face was bound in the fashion of death, her motion was as still as the grave, and well it might be, as it was nothing but a marble figure of some Grecian maid, long dead. We had one good laugh to reward the artist of so exquisite a piece of his skill. The young men went skipping down the hill towards our vessel. I, taking more interest in this monu-nental piece of affection, did not discover that my friends were gone until I found myself a "last Mohican." I started to descend the theatrical looking town, by winding in and out of small passage ways, until I found myself up an alley with no outlet, and when I turned to go out, the gate was fast and barred. A gate running in another direction was opened, and, old as a man could well be, was an old priest, seated on a stone beckoning to me to come in, I did not seem to comprehend, but he was determined I should, and came out with an extraordinary long string of beads nearly counted. He spoke several languages, and informed me that if my business was what all persons' business is that enter that alley, that he was ready to give me absolution. I informed him in French that I was there through a mistake ; and he then told me that it was usual in Syria for those wishing immediate absolution, to come to the priest's residence at all times, when there was no services in church, and on payment of a small fee, get value received in full. He was a kind old man. He offered to give me absolution right off, for any mistake, or bad intention that I allowed to occupy my attention, whilst in Syria.

Whilst I was explaining to the priest, I heard a suppressed laugh at the gate. The priest opened the gate and let me out. My friends were close by; they had seen me go in the passage way with no outlet and fastened the gate on me, as they say "to have a lark," but they little knew that they were then placing me in wisdom's way; I had

---

"last Mohican": A reference to James Fenimore Cooper's highly popular novel *The Last of the Mohicans*. The reference is casual and does not evoke the theme of being the last of a dying race.

learned more with the priest than I could from them all day long.

Our sail is up, and on ahead of us is Smyrna, the birth-place of Homer, one of the seven churches of Asia Minor, and it has 150,000 inhabitants, and it is close to the Isle of Patmos, where St. John wrote the Revelations and saw four angels standing on the four quarters of the globe holding up the four winds of Heaven, that they might not blow upon the sea nor the earth.

Smyrna has been destroyed ten or twelve times and still has a large population. Like Syra, Smyrna is on the side of a hill. None of its ancient buildings remain except a corner wall of an old church that resounded back the voice of St. John to the minds of his hearers, when he preached those very Epistles we hear every Sabbath, in all Christian lands. The streets and bazaars are densely crowded with business men from all smaller towns for hundreds of miles around, and the houses, which are only one story, seem to be as densely filled with pretty women. I see no window of a respectable looking house without a lady. I cannot describe the ladies dress as I was not fortunate enough to et inside, and as they are very seldom on the street. The dresses of the men were of so many styles it would not pay to describe them, it is enough to say that it consisted of a many colors as Joseph's coat, of some cotton or silk woof of all qualities.

There being no accommodation here for travelers, we did

not ask the captain to lay by all night. Next morning we
were sailing through the rapid Hellespont, at the Darden-
elles. About ten o'clock, A. M. we reached the part of the
Hellespont where Lord Byron swam across from Europe to
Asia — from Sestos to Abydos.

> " If in the month of dark December,
>   Leander, who was slightly wont
>   (What maid will not the tale remember?)
>   To cross thy stream, broad Hellespont!"

Here we stopped some minutes, and two or three yawls
came from the Asia side in quest of something to do. At
the hind part of one of these yawls was a large, fat and
shiney black African, doing the lazy part of the work—
steering. His heavy self weighed down the other end, containing two men and oars. It was a beautiful day and the
sun came down with a quivering heat in the distance, so, as
it is said, that the natives in the interior of Africa cook
their meat on sun heated rocks, he looked as if he was
about to broil. He attracted the attention and caused
amusement for the passengers; and some one threw some
orange peelings on his naked rotundity as he was half lying
on his back with no clothes on above his loins. He pre-
tended to take no notice of it until they came in such regu-
lar succession he could not but show signs of acknowledgement or cowardice. After his patience gave out, he turned
lazily around and looked up, like a duck at thunder, and
shook his head; they followed up this amusement until he

got agoing on the gibberish dialect, and that was more amusement yet; at last our boat left him, and one of our passengers translated his resentment. It was merely, "according to his ideas of decorum, he had not been treated gentlemanly, and that he would remember it if ever we came to his country, and that he would not consider us worth taking notice of."

On the morning of the 11th of May, the captain said to the sailors, "Bosphorus! down the hatch and bring the mail on deck." I looked ahead and saw an immense number of steeples, towers and minarets; to the eye no city on earth need look prettier. It was, indeed, the fairest sight I ever beheld. I asked an old Turkish tar what it was, he said, "Stamboul, stamboul." The captain said to the pilot, "right towards the Harem." Gondoliers from all directions of the "golden horn" were racing to us; in one of them a couple of officers, in their gay colors came. All our baggage was gondoliered, and we, all afloat, approached the Custom House. I slipped a five franc piece, as I had been told, in an officers hand, to get rid of the trouble of unlocking trunks, and he went blind, and I passed unmolested with my contraband, if I had any, into the great Mahommedan city, Constantinople.

THE DOGS PROVOKE ME, AND THE WOMEN ARE VEILED.

THE first visible annoyance in Constantinople is dogs, which Murray's guide says is nobody's property. In a space of a rod I counted seventy-four dogs, and not one respectable dog in the seventy-four! fifteen or twenty of them were marked on different parts of the body with scalds, some with only one ear, some blind, the streets were lined with them, lying down, standing up, fighting, breeding, and making love.   The Turks are as particular about getting around and through them, as a good man would be in a crowd of children; in fact, I saw a Turk tread upon a child in an effort to pass around dogs.   They take no notice o persons passing to and fro, but if you touch one, he jumps at you and lays hold.

During the night we have a long dog-note howl, from dark to daylight, and there is no way to stop it; they have systematical skirmishes of parties from different sections. Murray holds that they have fundamental laws of infringe-

---

Murray's guide: Murray's handbooks and guides to various European countries were extremely popular in the nineteenth century. Bayard Taylor writes disparagingly of travelers' reliance on Murray thus: "With Murray's Handbook open in their hands, they sat and read about the very towns and towers they were passing, scarcely lifting their eyes to the real scenes" (*Views A-Foot: Or, Europe Seen with Knapsack and Staff* [1848; Philadelphia: David McKay, 1890], 72).

ment, and woe be to him that don't acknowledge their legality. The puppies, as soon as they open their eyes, he observes, join in the first fight, and off goes his ear, tail, or leg, and he grows up used to hardships, and the customs and responsibilities of war; he is also taught the responsibility of invasion. Before he learns the landmarks, he goes on another's territory, where he is picked up by some old sentinel and shook a little, and thrown across the border, where he stands and barks a little, in defiance of the old dog's pluck and courage to come on this "spot and do the like. In their hymenial adventures" they frequently cross the borders, in pursuit of their object of affection, when there is a free fight, that lasts until some devoted amour falls a martyr to his sincerity, whilst the object of his affection escapes, heedless of his fidelity, and his great care for her and his posterity.

The virtue of keeping so many dogs in Constantinople, is to cleanse the streets of offal, that is piled there by the citizens, who are not blessed with sink holes under the streets, they empty their swill, bad vegtables, and scraps of all corruption in the middle of the streets, and the dogs act the buzzard's part, or the cholera would reign supreme all the year round. When the citizens are fearful of hydrophobia, the Sultan orders the dogs to be driven in herds to a lake a few miles from the city, and there to stay during the dog days; but when they are brought back, the city is generally raging with what they call in the east, the

---

Dorr's complaint about the dogs at Constantinople also echoes Nathaniel Parker Willis's. Willis wrote: "I had heard that the dogs of Constantinople knew and hated a Christian. By the time I had reached the middle of the square, a wretched puppy at my heels had succeeded in announcing the presence of a stranger. They were upon me in a moment from every heap of garbage and every hole and corner" (*Pencillings By the Way* [Philadelphia: Carey, Lea, and Blanchard, 1836], 52).

plague.   If the city was blessed with sink holes, they could then dispense with the nuisance of dogs in such narrow streets, and the provocation of their efforts of progeny. They are frequently so close together that a man hardly ever takes notice of their condition to one another. I, trying to pass through a group, got entangled between two and fell over them, as it was impossible to get through, as one tried to go one way, and the other another; I was so provoked when I got up, I did'nt look back to see whether it was their legs or tails was tied together; I am sure it was one or the other, from their magnanimous struggles to take one another their own way.

Another source of low spirits to a man from off the waters, is to see women moving about like spirits or shadows, and cannot be seen.   The promenades in Constantinople are the graveyards or any other sacred site.   The graveyards are like rustic parks with immense numbers of tombstones denoting the head of the grave, and all are inclined to a fall.   The ladies go there and lean against them and talk with their maids, and you can hear their sweet laugh, but see no smile.   They sit like a tailor, on the inside of their heels or ankles.   You will see five or six stand talking in their beautiful silk wrappers, and quick as a fall they will sink down upon those little feet, like a blossom sinking from its majesty of beauty to its downward decay.   They seem to get closer to the earth than any other people could. One nymph-like lady was so wiry in her manner of talking

---

women moving about like spirits: In concentrating on the veiled, covered women, Dorr is following the tradition of most travel writers, for whom harems and veiled women were metonyms for the Orient.

to her black maid, and so full of good humor, that I knew she must have been pretty. I looked at her one hour, and she at me, through her eyelits. I would have given five pds to lift her veil; I know she was pretty, her voice was so fluty, and her hands so delicate, and her feet so small, and her dress so gauzy; she was like an eel. I do not believe she had any bones in her. I asked the guide if there was no way in the world to get acquainted with her, and he said, none under heaven. The guide and myself moved along to see some others, and something new presented itself at every step. Vanity is reigning monarch in all females. I had stopped in another part of the graveyard pleasure ground, and whilst leaning against a tombstone, this Mohammedan maid came up and seated herself as near to me as she was before. Her maid had changed her veil, and was still fixing it on her mistress. This veil was thin enough to make me believe I could see her figure of countenance, and I swear she was pretty. The guide said that she was for sale, I told him to go and buy her for me, and asked him who owned her, he said, her mother, but I could not buy her because I was no Mohammedan. I asked him what did he think she was worth, he said, about a thousand Turkish piastres, a sum of about twenty-five dollars. I told him if he could buy her for that I would give twenty-five dollars for himself. This was a powerful engine on his reflective powers. He said he did not know how it could be done. I asked him if he thought the girl would admire me; he had no doubt about that, and added, I need not have any uneasiness about that, as I could make her love me after she was mine, she was obliged to obey me according to the Turkish laws, and no man could change the laws but Abdul Medjid, the Sultan.

A COLORED MAN FROM TENNESSEE SHAKING HANDS WITH THE SULTAN; AND MEN PUTTING WOMEN IN THE BATH AND TAKING THEM OUT.

FRIDAY is a festive day with the citizens of Stamboul. It is celebrated by gondolar rides along the canal called " sweet water." Males and females go up this canal, in all degrees of magnificence, and it is nothing but the elite of the city. From thirty to forty thousand assemble by eleven o'clock, the hour for the Sultan and his seven Sultanas, to arrive. Just about this hour it is very gay. The gentlemen are in groups of from two to ten, exercising on flageolets, or wooden or iron musical instruments of some kind. The ladies come some in Palanquins with strong Turks at each end, and others in a golden gilt carriage, drawn by either oxen, camels, or men; if oxen, their horns are decorated with ribbons and flowers, if camels no decoration of beauty is needed as they are appreciated for their capability of standing hardships and sufferings; if men, for their masculine limbs and jocular songs, whilst pulling the beauties to the festal scene.

Where I discovered the crowd thickest there I repaired, and the Mohammedans, were standing around a very large man, from Nashville, Tennessee, United States of America. His name was Frank Parish. He had in his hand as large a hickory stick as ever a man carried to be a stick; he wore Turkish costume from head to foot, and his Tarbouche was of the best red, and he stood up with a Narghehly in his hand and mouth, all cap a pie, *ala Turkoise*. Here the people began to give way for the Sultan and his seven legitimate wives. Frank didn't give way an inch of territory for the Sultan. Two or three Pachas rode a head of the Sultan seated on camels in their golden saddles. The Sultan stopped every fifty yards and listened to the music. When he stopped close to Frank, he cast his eyes on his great form, and seemed to be interested; and Frank had brass enough to look at the Sultan as he did at other people. Frank took his pipe from his mouth and walked up to the Sultan's carriage and offered his hand which the Sultan took, to the approbation of all present. The seven Sultanas were looking at Frank all the time through their eyelits as if they liked the looks of him. Frank is a man about 45 or 50 years of age, and looks like a man in every sense of the word. He is not a yellow, or black man, but what we call ginger-bread color. He had come to Constantinople, with a Mr. Ewing from Nashville, and was staying at Constantinople to recover from wounds he had received from Arabs that shot him through the shoulder with his own gun, whilst standing over the body of Mr. Ewing, who the Arabs were trying to kill, and thereby saved the life of Mr. Ewing. He was a free man and owned property in Nashville. The Sultan could plainly see that his loyal subjects were but as infants, by the giant-like man that stood over them. Being surrounded by such dwarf-like men, he showed off to great advantage. The Sultan is a weak looking man, and has the marks of fatigue well written on his forehead and limbs ; he also looks like a man surfeiting on the fat of the world. He is a slow walking man, and seems as if he experienced some weakness coming from a hidden source which allowed its approach so gradually and agreeable that he is not conscious of its fatality. He knows nothing of the rest of the world nor cares for it, but believes that himself and Constantinople are the wonders and powers of it.

He is only twenty-two years old, but never once has been out of his Paradise, Shamboul. According to his opinion, he has no equals, consequently he has no associates. He is uneducated, because no one dare to instruct him.. Such a man lives a Monarch and will die like a fool. If the Czar of Russia were to pay him a visit, he might smile with acknowledgement, but if Queen Victoria's virtuous head would call, she could not stop in his seraglio as quick as Madame Rachel or Lolla Montez ; and if General Zack

---

Madame Rachel or Lolla Montez: Lola Montez was a famous dance hall singer in Germany. Her affair with King Louis I of Bavaria contributed to the Revolution of 1848. Madame Rachel was a famous actress. She was brought to Paris in 1830 and appeared in many successful performances. She visited London, Brussels, Berlin, and St. Petersburg, meeting enthusiastic applause everywhere.

Taylor called, his Pacha's would receive him, and a General Jackson would scare him to death, as he is the most nervous man on a Throne.

As he is the descendant of Mahommed, it is admitted here that his authority to govern the people is received on all emergencies from God. He is incapable of fearing any nation on the earth, as he thinks that his is head of all. If some day, the news went to his palace that the Bosphorus was covered with a fleet, and that one ball had already struck the dome of the mosque St. Sophia, he would, through all his resolutions, break his haughty heart, and no doubt tremble off his divan. They are talking about a war with Russia, and I can find no man here that thinks Russia can begin to fight them.

The Sultan's harems are numerous. While the occupants of the large are removed to two small ones, we have permission to pass through it, to see its magnificence, by paying the sum of five dollars a piece. It is a government of itself. It has a large bath room of water, and one of vapor. The girls are as pure as silvan nymphs, and some have remained in this harem until they become old, on account of the Sultan's fancy to certain ones. They are carried to the baths by black men, called eunuchs. They take their baths in all attitudes of pleasure, while these eunuchs lean over the large, stationary stone basins, and gaze at them in their Eve like costumes. But before these men are placed in this important position of servitude, they are privately handled to the disadvantage of displaying any demonstrations of manly pride, towards these vexed reflections that must naturally spring up in the reflective minds of virgins deprived of the luxuries of a life, built upon the confines of clandestine border thoughts of *sexes*.

GOING TO ATHENS WITH A PRIMA DONNA.

HAVING seen the Sultan's great City, mosques, ambers, sponges, perfumeries and beads, I am now passing the Custom House, on my way back to Greece.

In the front part of this vessel the cabin is all one, and whoever gets any kind of a berth is lucky, as the passengers are numerous. The beds or berths are one over the other, like our lake boats' second class cabin. One berth is a little higher than the other, they are three stories, and one person has to climb over another to get in bed, and even then you are too close together. The second class passengers find their own bedding, and sleep upon deck, and we have some very rich Greecian families aboard, with their bedding and food, who sleep on deck. Yesterday we passed by Smyrna, and stopped and took aboard three beautiful Albanian girls. When you see a pile of old rubbish lying about on these Dardanelle boats, there is always some owner lying under it.

These Albanian girls were dressed very different from the

Turkish girls, and the pretty ones are not veiled. They had on a very pretty costume, but over it they wore a very large and coarse cloak, composed of either camel's hair, or wool of some ugly animal. They have a bonnet attached to it, that they can either throw back, or wear on their heads, and this cloak drags the ground. On board of our vessel was two young gentlemen from New York, trying to attract the attention of these Albanian girls, though they had their beaux with them. These young gents are very rich, their wholesale oil establishment, in New York, is said to do a business of millions of dollars per annum, and their names were Bridgers. They were seen to follow these beauties wherever they promenaded the deck, still they received no encouragement. Sometimes these girls would hide themselves in their winding sheet, and throw the bonnet part over their heads, and fall down upon the deck as singular and as natural as an apple from a tree, and then they would appear as a pile of rubbish of old sacks. At last the gay Messrs. Bridgers lost them, and they hunted in all directions, but could not find these fairies. They got tired hunting, and seated themselves to talk on some old piles of blankets and quilts, but before he got seated. I mean only one, he was thrown flat on his face by one of these pretty girls. In choosing a comfortable seat, he picked the covered head of the prettiest girl. He felt very bad about the mistake he had made, and I felt ashamed for him, but worst of all, he could make no amends, as she spoke nothing but Greek.

He said " I wish I could apologize," but he could'nt.   She did not seem to like it at all.

The first night out we had a good deal of contention about berths. We had more passengers than the law of this company allows; they are not allowed to take one passenger more than they can accommodate.

Among the passengers on board was the first dancer of Constantinople.   Those who had spoken for berths went to bed soon for fear disputes would arise about the right of them.   I made sure of mine by sitting by it and watching it. After all the berthers had taken possession of their respec- tive places, I discovered many persons taking berths on the sofas around the cabin ; there were some curtains hanging about to make screens, to dress and undress behind, and the lights always burned dimly.   These sofas were on a level with the lower berths, consequently, whoever took a sofa berth, was almost sleeping with the occupant of the lower berth.

There was some choice about them, inasmuch as some were wider than others.   I could see through my thin curtain that some one had picked out X 31, my own doorway.   I lay like a rock to find out who it was, until I saw that everybody was in a resting attitude, after which I quietly drew back my curtain, to see what my neighbor was like.   I knew it was some respectable person from the sweet smell of roses and other eastern scents which I inhaled.   I could dimly see a Madonna figure of considerable size, and the figure was nearly touching me. I did not get scared but lay as quiet as possible. I saw plainly that sleep had sent in a regret for that night, the lamp flickered up and went down, leaving a dark twilight perceptible around the cabin, and I put my hand slowly out to see what my neighbor felt like, and I felt the veritable prima donna of Constantinople, "*qu est ce que vous voulez,*" said she, "*rien,*' said I, and shut my eyes and went to sleep in a hurry, and slept as sound as any man could, by the side of a live Prima Donna.

"qu est ce que vous voulez": What do you want?
"rien": Nothing.

ATHENS, A SEPULCHRE.

WHEN Rome had a Cæsar and a Cicero, and a Cassius with a Brutus, Athens dictated the arts and sciences for her. Though she cannot claim the originality of them, she can the perfection of beautifying. The conquest of Alexander the Great, in Egypt, among the Africans, was considered the greatest triumph of conquest ever made by man, because it enabled the warlike people of Greece, to adorn their triumphs with the spoils of the vanquished. Egypt was a higher sphere of artistical science than any other nation on the earth. This will naturally convey an idea to the world that the black man was the first skillful animal on the earth, because Homer describes the Egyptians as men with wooly hair, thick lips, flat feet, and black, and we have no better authority than Homer. We know not the exact epoch of his time, but we know it was before any other authentic chronicler, save the sacred book of Moses, by the fact that he voyaged on the Nile before the pyramids were built, which we can trace three thousand years.

Homer describes the Egyptians as men with wooly hair: Once again, Dorr is entering the intense debates about Egyptology and race that raged in the mid-nineteenth century. The African features of the Sphinx, in particular, caused consternation to ethnographers like Samuel George Morton, who published his findings in *Crania Aegyptica* (1844) and George R. Gliddon and Josiah C. Nott, who sought to disprove the connection in their immensely popular work, *Types of Mankind* (1854). For further discussion of Egyptology and racial classification in the nineteenth century, see Malini Johar Schueller, *U.S. Orientalisms: Race, Nation, and Gender in Literature, 1790–1890* (Ann Arbor: University of Michigan Press, 1998), 33–38.

On the 29th of May, 1852, as the sun was going down the blue arch of the western sky, I reached the top of Mars Hill, in Athens, and seated myself in the seat where St. Paul rested from his display of power over a bigoted people, when he said, "I perceive that in all things you are too snperstitious."

When St. Paul stood on Mars Hill, Athens was a voluptuous city to look at. There was the white marble temple of Apollo, Jupiter, Minerva, Juno and Mars, besides temples to the sun and moon, and one to the " unknown god," all of which were reared up in the most conspicuous reigns of those gods over the minds of all the inhabitants of Athens in a limited degree. As I descended Mars Hill, I turned to the right and entered the temple of Bacchus, who is described in the classical dictionary thus : " son of Jupiter and Semele, and god of wine and drunkards, nourished till a proper time of birth in his fathers thigh, after the death of his mother, whom Jupiter, at her request, visited in all his majesty. Semele, who was a mortal and unable to bear the presence of a god, was consumed to ashes." An old man was in the temple to keep people from breaking pieces off from the beautiful temple's treasure, which was the tomb of Bacchus, with the god carved on the sides, drinking his delight. I did not know what god's temple this was, and enquired of the old man, he could not speak any European language, but was quite successful in conveying the information I wanted; he took an old gourd and scooped some water up from the bottom of a bucket, and drank it with great hilarity, at the same time pointing to Bacchus, as if he would say, "he drank!" I said, "You mean to say this is the temple of Bacchus, the god of wine and drunkards, do you?" he bowed towards his toes and then stood erect, and tried to make me understand that the rest of the tombs there were gods and goddesses, of which Apollo loved either sexually or valorously. There were no windows to the temple, the only inlet was the door, but though the door was shut, it was as light inside as one would wish. The marble was transparent, and when the sun shone upon its roof or walls, it forced its light through in a determined way.

As I left this veritable tomb and sepulchre of the great god of wine and drunkards, my guide pointed to an aperture from the heart of a hill, and said, that entrance goes to the cave where Socrates was poisoned. We then went up the most imposing ruins of Athens, the Acropolis. The temples there looked down upon the rest of the temples of Athens, like Jupiter would at the feast of gods, it was higher and more stupendous than all. There was the seats of solid blocks of white marble of the twelve judges. They were all in a row, and only one broke. They were solid blocks with scooping apertures, for a man to place his rotundity in comfortable quarters. Round about the ruins were balls and cannon, grape, and several bursted shells, but one half of this tremendous mass of splendid ruins stood upright, as when it first took its stand among the wonders of the world, as a temple of wisdom. This temple makes it impossible for us to pronounce ourselves the "light of all ages."

The great god of this temple was the Ammon of the Africans, the Belus of the Babylonians and the Ossiris of the Egyptians; from him, mankind receives his blessings, and their blessings of miseries, and he is looked upon as one acquainted with everything, past, present and future. Saturn was Jupiter's father, and conspired against his son and in consequence was banished from his kingdom. Now Jupiter became ruler of the universe and sole master of the Empire of the world, and divided with his brothers, reserving for himself the kingdom of heaven, and giving the Empires of the sea to Neptune, and that of the infernal regions to Pluto. The sea moved at his wrath, and hell burned his opposers, and he looked down from heaven at the commotion of his wrath till the men on earth considered their welfare only secured by worshipping his smile. Athens and all her superstition is gone now, and the godly man now laughs at the folly of the wisdom that all talent of old times craved for. On Mars hill where St. Paul thundered the decrees of God against gods, though nothing

to designate the spot, there the Christian of to-day would
rather stake his salvation than from the most sacred abode
of Jupiter and Juno. But there is still weak minds in
Athens, for as I descend I see on the side of a hill that
celebrated stone where females used to come from all parts
of Italy as well as Greece to slide down on it, as a true
avoidance of barrenness. This stone is as slick as a piece of
soap, so slick a lizzard could not run down it. For nearly
three thousand years two and three thousand women per
day have slid down it in a sitting posture. The guide
books call it the "substitute rock for female barrenness."
Many a bruise has this rock given in receiving its polish.
Hundreds of boys and young men are here at present,
sliding down it for fun.

I see, seated about fifty feet away from it, the Tennessee
negro I described at Constantinople, Frank Parish, A
Scotchwoman is seated beside him, and seems to be proud
of him as a beaux. She is a lady's maid that came here
yesterday from the Sublime Porte with her mistress and
Frank. The Scotch lady insisted on Frank taking a slide
with the young men, but for Frank it was no joke, as he
was an extraordinary large man. But Frank, being as
full of conspicuousness as any other man, it only
required a little coaxing to get him started; at last he
seated himself for a slide, but he did not much like to let
go lest there would be a crash up. He anchored himself to

Sublime Porte: The office of the Grand Vizier was known as the Sublime
Porte; he acted as mayor of Constantinople as well as deputy Sultan.

the top and hesitated some, paused and looked like a fool. An Irish servant that was with the same family as the Scotchwoman, encouraged Frank, by saying, "be a marn," Frank said, "if I am not a man there is none about here," just to fill up the pause of suspense; but while Frank was looking and studying, the Irishman loosened his hands, and he went down like a colossus; seeing that he had broke no bones, he got up with a smile and felt himself all over to see if he was safe and sound. The Irishman said, "how did it feel my marn?" Frank pronounced it the most pleasant sensation he ever experienced. "Then ye never dreamed that ye were married," said the Irishman. Frank said he had, but had forgot it. The Scotchwoman wished to know if that was a pleasant dream; the Irishman said, "it was the most pleasant dream a marn could have, and the most unpleasant was to find it a lie."

Starting from the "female substitute for barrenness," we met a man with a telescope, and we all wanted to take a fair view of Athens. The Irishman borrowed it from the man and took the first squint. He pointed to a fine house towards the Kings palace, and there he looked alone. When I obtained it I looked there too, and saw a beautiful Grecian maid combing her long black hair; gazing at her until she finished, I got a most ungentlemanly view of a lady, from which, in all due respect to her, I had to refrain, and took another direction in search of fair views.

"if I am not a man there is none about here": It is important to note that Dorr emphasizes Frank Parish's masculinity or "being a man." Since white masculinity meant the privilege of paternity, ownership, and power, attempting to gain a culturally sanctioned form of masculinity meant gaining a sense of power and control.

We went down the hill, and as we moved along the Grecian ladies' and gentlemen's walks, I, though mixed up in a crowd of different people, was determined to hear Frank talk to this Scotchwoman. He was telling her of his business, which was still going on in Nashville, Tennessee, and of how many improvements he intended to make in his bath house and barber shop, when he returned, with things that he had already bought in Paris. She believed it all, and Frank was in his glory. I noticed their actions particularly, and was upon the eve of hearing their loveliest words, when she stopped as if it was a great sacrifice to her to give up his company. They lingered some time, as they would fain go on, but as she was going to her mistress' hotel, and Frank to his, they must part. Frank was well versed for the occasion, in Byron. He took her by the hand and looked her in the face affectionately, and said with emotion,

> " Maid of Athens, ere we part,
> Give, oh give me back my heart."

As Frank was going to my hotel I thought it well to make his acquaintance; he said he saw me at Constantinople, but as I was an American, he did not deem it necessary to make my acquaintance, as I knew that he was a mere barber from Tennessee. He also told me he had been married several times, and was now engaged at home. The day after this, I was outside of Athens at what is called " the amusement grounds " of Athens, for the people repair there every evening to hear the national band play. This band comes from Bavaria, where Greece got her present king. King Otho is the son of the King of Bavaria. Here the king rides out every evening, and here Frank took another liberty with royalty. As the King and his wife rode up to the band, his horses stopped just at Frank's elbow, and Frank walked to the carriage and offered his red hand to the king, and it was, through courtesy, accepted. Athens is to-day a small town, and the King lives here. The whole population of Greece is not quite a million. Our slaves would make four kingdoms as powerful in population as Greece. Oh, when will we be the "Freest government in the world?" We looked from the Acropolis down upon a village, but in old times we looked upon a town. "Ah! Greece, they love thee least who owe thee most." The women are still pretty, and what is like a Grecian nose? Come, pilgrim, and see Athens in the days when it is not even a shadow of its former greatness, and ask yourself if power constitutes stability. Yes, go upon the Acropolis and gaze downward to the top of Mars' hill, and look at the council stand of St. Paul; raise your eyes and turn them eastward, and if your imagination is as good as your sight, you will see the sea that in old times was covered over with the fleet of Alexander the Great. Further off from the shore, in the year of our Lord 1191, Richard I. of England, the lion-hearted, crusaded along with men, women, children, cattle and dogs, to put down infidelity on the sacred plains of Palestine, where Abraham, Isaac and Jacob walked as types of moral light for the salvation of mankind. Now, as you stand there on the Acropolis, as Cecrops himself has stood, be not disgusted at what you see below, of the so much written of towns, for though now you see Athens, it is true you do not see herself, but "Athens a sepulchre."

BEAUTIFUL VENICE.

ON a little slip of land between the gulf of Lepante and Athens, we come to Corinthe; we know it not, save a few immense pillars of marble pinnacling the site of Corinthe. Artists from all parts of the world come here and sit down at their base to sketch their dimensions; then away they go, with no regretful feelings for the great founders of arts stupendous, who, perhaps, three thousand years ago, were known far and near as men of the best faculties. The greatest gem that Rome ever put in its crown, was the one that was made by imagination of the Greecian dictator when listening to Cicero, he said, "Rome has robbed us of all we possess, but our eloquence, and it seems as if that is going towards Rome." But Rome has since fallen as low as Athens!

In the Ionian sea, between Sicily and Greece, are the Ionian islands, seven in number, and Corfu is the principal one; they now all belong to the English. Out further

the East Indias, where the the queen of England has
150,000,000 subjects; on the coast of Africa, at the cape of
Good Hope, the West Indias, and the Canadas, is her scep-
tral wand waving its ambrosial food of civilization. "The
sun never sets on the Queen's domain."

Between Asia, Macedonia, and Greece is the most celebrated archipelago in the world. Six days along the Adriatic
have brought me to Trieste, in Northern Italy. It now
belongs to Austria. The Austrian sceptre is waving
over nearly half of Italy. It is generally believed she
cannot much longer hold her Italian possessions. The army
of Austria, like its eagle's wings, is stretched to its utmost
extremity of space. She could not sustain 50,000 more
troops, without breaking some of her internal machinery.
Like an overflowing river, she is most too high to rise any
higher without damaging her Union. She seems to have
taken the last drop of the Italian's patience and forbearance,
while Leghorn, Lucca, Trieste, Venice, and other Italian
cities, and other foreign powers, are trying to overflow her
channels of power; they are perfectly willing that these
troubled waters should spread across the plain of the Hapsburg policy, and turn the institution of tyranny from
Hungary, Bohemia, and Italy; but the beardless, blue-eyed
Emperor seems to be as undisturbed as a god of liberty, and
heedless of the consequences of a rebellion of these warlike people. Five hours' ride from Trieste is Venice, a city

the Hapsburg policy . . . blue-eyed Emperor: In 1848, uprisings by
Bohemia, Italy, and Hungary were suppressed by the Hapsburgs of
Austria. The emperor of Austria at the time was eighteen-year-old Franz
Josef.

in the sea. More lovely cities, perhaps, have been built, but I have never seen them. As our steamer threw out her anchor about fifty yards from the city, I could see on the other side of the city, a railroad in the sea, and cars running along as the sea spray washed their sides. On all sides gondolas were racing toward us, which we went ashore in. This magnificent city is built in the sea, and it costs more to drive down piles, in Venice, to build a house, than it costs in London or Paris to build the whole house.

There is one building in this city of the sea, more beautiful inside, in its old age, than most of the best buildings of its kind, in any kingdom in the world, are in when they are new. It is the church of St. Mark. The body of St. Mark is in its cloisters, resting in his magnificent tomb, like a sleeping giant that dare not be aroused. The floor of this old gothic building is precious stones ; the pillars near the alters are alabaster. The Pope, in the Doge days of Venice, put his foot upon the Emperor Alexander's head. All the magnificent displays of state, even in these times, cannot be worthy of the notice of the people of this part of the world, unless it be the will of the Pope ; he is much feared by the monarch's of to day. It has been proven that the Napoleon of to day has been seeking the smile of Pius IX. It seems very strange to some people, but not to me, that the kings of England and France, in the eleventh century, should hold the Pope's horse for him to alight.

While walking around the church of St. Mark, I saw a beautiful figure of a woman leaning gracefully from a stool downward. I watched her to see if any miracle was about to be performed. I saw the beautiful creatnre move with a blush upon her cheek. She was confessing to an old father, of whom, I saw, was more partial than moral worth sanctions, for as soon as she left the box, another made application, but the priest took no notice of it, but walked into his vestry. The applicant was an old woman, and homely as a bone, which, I have no doubt, was qualifications for religion not comporting with his reverence's sensitive taste of moral obligation, to receive confessions from so ugly a source to fill up the ranks of his beautiful herds. This poor old woman waited some time for his return, but like gifts from lips that frequent promise, he never came.

This church is attached to the palace of the great Doge of Venice, and across a canal that runs between this palace and the prison, is a bridge. When a culprit was judged and sent across this bridge, he never saw again his 25th hour. All the instruments the ingenuity of man could invent, is here found to destroy the human body. I saw one machine to put a man in, and gradually break his bones; at the crush of each bone, he would be asked "if he would confess the crime?" Another was a steel covering for a man's head, with seven holes in it; the culprit's head would be firmly placed in this iron case, whilst he would be seated on an iron block, one nail would gradually be driven in at a time, until all the seven holes would be filled with long nails, meeting in the centre of the head, unless he confessed his guilt when some of the nails were hammered down. Another machine was something like a brace for the loins, and each end came curve like together and left it in'the shape of a hoop; it had a lock and key, and old tyrannical lords used it when they left home, to protect their wives' virtue. He would put it around below the loins, lock it, put the key in his pocket, and go out hunting. No man could unlock it, and in those times false keys were not so easily obtained as now. When he returned he would unlock it, as he could then keep guard over her to his own satisfaction.

From this horrid place, reader, come with me down the great canal that traverses the whole town, with its branches, to where, at from ten to one o'clock every day, would meet together the "merchants of Venice." Here their financiering would daily rock thrones, but now you see a long row of decaying old walls whose bases are wrapt in sea-weed, like climbing serpents, that now dwell in those damp, old commercial halls, now rotting away. I asked the guide for the site of Desdemona's father's house, but that was forgotten.

Here we find no horses, carriages, or cars, but myriads

of gondolas intercept the traveler at every turn of an alley or canal. On a beautiful moonlight night, I went through the city in my gondola, and as my oar struck the salty brine fiercely, I could see myriads of lights reflected from the various built palaces, and the sea looked like a diamond lawn.

VERONA AND BOLOGNA.

ONE morning, at sunrise, I was rapidly roaring towards the depot that was to carry me to Verona. All was lone and still, for the Venicians are no early risers. As still as the zephyr wind gondolas passed by me, and away the ripples flew. I left this city in the sea, and about ten o'clock arrived at Verona; a city so handsome in appearance —so magnificent in its ruins—so picturesquely situated in a plain, I felt as if I could dwell an age with it. Having obtained a cicerone we repaired to the old ruined walls of Julliete's fathers' house; afterwards the old man insisted on us going to see the half of her tomb, which is still preserved. No traces can be found of Romeo or his father's house or tomb.

In Verona is many beautiful churches, the principal of which is San Zenone. San Zenone was a black man, and was the patron of Verona. He is represented as seated in a chair, with costly robes around him; his face is the picture of gloom, whilst his brow is stern and commanding. Preparations were going on for the reception of one of the oldest Bishops of Italy. The church was thrown wide open and workmen were employed in all parts of the inside of this edifice. Behind the altar, was preserved some holy water, brought from Rome for the occasion. The priest poured some out of the jug into a tin bucket and gave it to one of his boy aids to pour in the basin found at the entrance to all Catholic churches. This little priest boy returned to the vestry for more, received it, but when he returned to the basin where he had deposited the first bucket full, he discovered that the basin was minus the first bucket of water. His great amazement scared even the workmen. He returned to the priest and informed him that some unforeseen cause had deprived the church of the precious libation. The priest soon discovered the pheno-menon, and pronounced it an omen unfavorable to the reception of the great bishop on his way here. It was talked about town that day, that the great bishop could not be received in the aisles of San Zenone. But I saw a thirsty boy looking in at the door, go up to the basin and drink his fill of the holy water, brought from Rome in a jug, and pronounced it not so good as he thought it was, by a jug full. I told the proprietor of the hotel that a boy drank the water, and he said, "I must be mistaken, as no one in Verona was so ignorant as to quench thirst on holy

water." Some said it was the devil thirsting for the protection of San Zenone, for no admirer that hoped for salvation by the intercession of this holy saint, would be guilty
of such a rash act, as they could not expect him to intercede
in behalf of the spoilers of his festivals, unless their admiration of him was so great that they felt it their duty to
partake of his blessings beyond the power of their resist-
ance, even of stealing them.

On my way to the railroad station, I passed the amphi-
theatre, that, in the gladiatorial days of Verona, held one
hundred thousand persons in its arena, and where they
saw the lion tear the man, and again where the man slew
the lion. That same night I slept at Mantua, one of the
most strongly fortified towns of Italy, and from here I went
to Bologna and bought a sausage. This is a beautiful town
so far as churches and graveyards add to the beauty of
towns, and the latter is more extensive than the former.
I informed the landlord of the hotel Europe that I needed
a guide for at least a day. He went in search of one and
returned with a schoolmaster, who had closed his school of
fifty scholars, to wait on us at the enormous sum of one
ducat per day. This was a little pert man with a body
twice as long as his legs. "Gentlemen," said he, "let us
be moving, there is a great deal to be seen before nightfall
in Bologna." I informed him that I wanted to see one of
the sausage manufactories, but he seemed to be ignorant

that Bologna was celebrated in the sausage line. He asked some wayfaring man through those old lonesome streets to tell him where sausage was made. After seeing the manufactory and the lean donkeys, he took me to see a gymnasium, and here I saw the insignia of every organized people on the earth except my own, and looking for our eagle, stars and stripes, without finding them, I asked him how it was they could not be found. He said this institution was ten years old, to his certain knowledge, and as we were a new people and country, he supposed this was the reason. Bologna, like a candle, must soon be extinguished for want of fuel of such combustibles as will burn up the dark ignorant pile now hid from the bright light that ought to shine supreme from the temple of wisdom of the times.

Venice, with her sea bathed palaces, may survive it, as she is still in beauty the "pride of the sea," more so than Bologna is the pride of graveyards, churches and sausage. The "Two Young Men of Verona" is better known to the world to-day than Verona or Bologna.

FIRENZA DE BELLA CITA.

WHEN we were within two hours drive of Florence, the Capitol of Tuscany and as it is also called the "Italian Capitol of fine arts," we stopped at a hotel to dine and feed horses. The landlord having ascertained that we might probably feel like paying something for what he called dinner, came into the sitting room with a live chicken by the neck and wished to know if I would order something to eat; I answered in the affirmative, when he gave his arm a twist and off went the chicken from his head, fluttering into nonentity. I informed mine host that the stage would hardly wait so long as was necessary to prepare the fowl, and he said he knew more about that than I did. A few moments after this he returned with the crawling flesh of the chicken, some wine and bread, as if he had done something really worth mentioning, and said, "now sir, here is some as fresh chicken as you ever eat, I am not like those town hotels that allow every thing to rot and stink before they sell it." A beautiful Italian girl that was a passenger

---

Firenza de Bella Cita: Florence, the beautiful city.

in the dilligence with me, was waiting to get something, and she said to me " you sir, seem to be the lucky one." I thought it proper to give some one a small piece of the fresh chicken, but if she had not been so pretty she might have been the " unlucky one." Up over the door of this man's house was written, these German words, *Gasthof Zum New York*. It not taking as much time to dine in the Gosthof as in the stable, we took a walk to see the extraordinary phenomena of a muddy place that one can set a blazing with a match. Having arrived at Florence and hoteled myself I ascertained where the races were, and was told they would commence in thirty minutes and that my hotel window was as good a seat at the races as I could get. I looked out of the window and saw the streets clean as a floor of a log cabin, and written upon the corner "Course." That was the name of the street. A few minutes after the heralds proclaimed " that this course must be cleared " as round at the stand the horses were on the track. This street is circular, and the horses run round, till they come to where they start from, when the race is awarded to the first that comes. No riders are allowed, but the people which makes a paling round the track, hurry each horse on. The horses don't seem to know they are running a race, because the shouts of the populace at every window, corner and alley is so frightening they are trying all the time to get out of the track

Before the races commence, a carriage with four greys is conveying an old man and wife up a street that comes to the course and branches off, and after the race, himself and lady is the first to ride on the street called *"la course;"* and after his carriage every other person has a right to enter the promenade of this man and wife, the Grand Duke, of Tuscany. In the next carriage to his was a tall lady with a beaux by her side, who, I learned, was the Princess, his daughter. Next to her carriage, was a Mr. Bullion from California, trying to pass himself off for a real American gentleman. These are the times when men who make money in the Eldorado, come home to the States to show off. He certainly had more money than brains. He had a liveried carriage. The smoke curled up in little clouds behind him, his feet were on the fore cushion of the open Calashe, and a profusion of beard adorned all the lower extremity of his face. His beard reminded me of Col. May's the captor of La Vega. The Duke halted a moment causing all in the train to halt also, when Mr. B. rose up in his carriage and looked round the Dukes carriage and told his driver to drive on He was informed that he could not, and he looked up very wise as if he would like to know why. A few minutes after the train moved, and he said to his driver "wait a little, I don't want them to think I want to follow them." The driver stopped and got himself in trouble, for the vehicle behind him told him to

drive on or get out of their way.   Here the Police inter-
feared and ordered Mr. consequence Bullion Esq., of the
El Dorado to get out of the way of gentlemen and ladies.
He tried to pursuade the officers to bear in mind he was
talking to an American citizen; but there was as much
difference as space between the Torrid and Frigid Zone.
The officer gave him to understand that he might be a
Florentine, but he must get out of the way of other people.
Mr. B. spit a mouthful of juice in the carriage, threw his
feet on the front cushion and told the driver to go on.   At
first my national pride was somewhat lowered, but on second
thought, I gloried in knowing that Americans are not
responsible for every upstart that goes abroad and violates
the rules and regulationss of other communities because
they were not made to suit his taste, for which no body ever
cared but himself.   The good people of Europe know full
well that there is always thistles among roses and not all
good among themselves.

American people are not as selfish as Italians.   Italians
will hate a man for ever for a Paul or Bioca.   I got acquainted with an Italian at the work shop of Hiram Powers,
and this young man volunteered to show me Florence, which
would of course save me the expense of a lacquey; and my
old lacquey told me he wished this man was dead, as he had
deprived him of a Ducat.   An English writer, tells a tale
on Fontenelle thus: "He once ordered some asparagus

cooked in oil for his dinner, for he was passionately fond of it; in five minutes afterwards, an abbey came to see him on some church politics, and as it is usual in France to ask ones friend how he wishes his dinner cooked and name what you have, Fontenelles told the old man what he had, and the old man said he would have half of the asparagus cooked in butter. Fontenelles thought it a great sacrafice, but said nothing. Thirty minutes afterward the abbey's valet came down in the parlor and exclaimed in great sorrow that while the abbey was washing he was taken with an apilepic fit and was dead. Fontenelles struck the youth on the shoulders and said, " run to the kitchen and tell the cook, to cook all the asparagus in oil." Now this was indeed a selfish man. Sam Slick asked a country beaux " why it was that such a fine looking gentleman as himself was not married where so many pretty ladies were ?" His answer was " when I offer my hand to a lady, she will be a lady ! " This is another selfish man. An Irishman once drinking his neighbors wine was too selfish to testify his approbation of its merrits, by drinking a toast of such good wine to his neighbor. At last he was compelled to drink one, and he said, " here is to my wifes husband." The French is celebrated for eating, the Yankee for his pride, and Irishmen for their toddies.

> ".The lads and lasses blightly bent,
> To mind both soul and body,
> Set round the table weel content
> And steer about the toddy."

But I have never found even wit, to justify an Italian's selfishness, only sublimity of meanness is an Italian's selfishness.

BACK TO PARIS

On my departure from Florence, I luxuriated at Lucca, the bathing resort of the Tuscans. The city is old with stout walls around it. Three hours ride in a viturino will bring you to the baths. They are beautifully located, down in a valley with craggy and fertile mountains hanging over. It was quite a place in old times, and Counts, and Dukes and other nobles used to flock here to gamble, until so much murder was committed, Lucca broke up the resort of these monied men, and until very recently it was thought to be destroyed and dead, but the Austrians, who occupy all the important places in the government of this part of Italy, wishing to resurrect something that has already been in the Italians' mind as a pleasant dream, hotels have been built, and livery stables erected, for the accommodation of the gay portion of Florence, Pisa, Genoa, Leghorn, and even Milan. On my way from Florence to Lucca I stopped at Pisa. Pisa is well known to the world as holding up one of the seven wonders of the world, to the world's travelers and sight seers. I have reference to the "leaning tower." In describing the "leaning tower," I will merely say, that the first vast and solid layer of stone is heavy enough to hold all the others laid upon it. Each layer is fastened to the one under, and though it might protrude several feet on the layers protruding side, this few feet of reaching out stone can have no power over all the rest of that same layer around this immense tower. The next layer protrudes on the same perched side of the tower, and straight over the reaching edge of its under layer,; as each layer is fastened with iron spikes to its under layer, there can be no chance of even the very top falling down on the side of the tower. It leans so much on each layer as to make the top of the tower reach away over the base on the leaning side, so much so that, were it to break loose, it would fall over to the earth without touching the base or foundation of the leaning side of the tower.

The City of Pisa is well known in Italian history, by the awful contentions that used to exist among next door neighbors. Men used to fight on the top of their own houses, and go on conquering, from house to house, until they would slay as many as twenty lords, whose property would be theirs as spoils of war. One hour and a quarter's ride from Pisa is Leghorn, a city full of hats and bonnets. The bay is dotted over with little white houses, and some miles out in the sea; and I see hundreds of small boats rowing towards bath houses. The strongest merchants here are English, who ship Leghorn hats and bonnets to foreign ports, as well as their own, but the city belongs to the Hapsburg sceptre, and thousands of Austrian soldiers stand in the by ways of public places.

Twelve hours travel through the sea from here, brought me to the "City of Palaces," Genoa. It is a city on the side of a hill, with eight story palaces looking down on the sea. Before the fifteenth century it had the inducement for traders that Lyons to-day has. Silk was manufactured here in a way that astonished that age of pride; but since the invention of steam, all those scientific arts that this trade called for is but as nothing, and Italians look at our steam power machines, and then at all their scientific arts, and like the proud fowl that gazed downward, their feathers fall.

I must now pass over many places and their accomplishments, and hasten back to France, to prepare myself for the roughest voyage yet—Egypt, Arabia and Palestine. Here is the Pyramids, Memphis, (now Cairo) Thebes, the Nile, the Red sea, the desert of Sahara, Mount Sinai, the tomb of Abraham, Isaac, Jacob and Joseph, at Hebron, the city of David; and to Jerusalem, down to Jericho where the Jordan's muddy waters slip under the briny and sulphurous liquid of the grave God dug for Sodom and Gomorrah; and to Olives, Carmel, Tabor and Calvary; and to Damascus, the Cedars of Lebanon, Nazareth, Bethel, and the temple of Balbec or Baal.

Prussia, Bavaria, Sardinia and Saxony I will pass through without comment, more than to say that I found them separate nations of one people, save in language. However, I will say, that of all the German kingdoms the most despotic is Austria; but she hates slavery more than the "freest government in the world." Austria tyrannizes over man, but she cannot tyrannize, chattelize, and prostrate their rights with impunity, any more than Washington, Jefferson, or Henry could.

EGYPT AND THE NILE.

FIVE months of Paris life is again spent, and with it winter has gone by. Winter takes away and deadens the energies of a gay man, but the spring time comes, and with it the awakening of man from his lethargy, and like old Sol from the bed of the sea, in his majesty he shakes himself in all his rising glory, and puts a fiery garb between himself and all the rest of creation, to scorch the temptation that would impede his bright and manly career. Did you ever stand by the shore of a bed of water, reader, and see old Sol, like a mighty giant, rise up from his wet pillow, and seem to shake his shaggy locks, as they loosened from the abode of Neptnne fcr more etherial spheres, and when at his journey's end, fall again on his pillow of the watery down? If you have, see me alike pulling away from the festal abode of Paris' comfort, and loosening the tie of familiar smiles, for a hard journey over

a rough sea, dead lands, and a treacherous people. Will I
not be willing, as old Sol when he fell on the western sea,
to rest my mortal part on the flinty base of great Pompey's
pillar, ere the work be "did and done?" I think I will! I
have passed Marseilles, Malta in the sea, and here I am in
sight of land. Well, Mr. Captain, what are you looking
after in the distance with as much anxiety as the passengers,
have you not been here before? "Yes sir, but every body
wants to see Pompey's pillar." "That's a fact, Captain, is
that his pillar?" At this stage of the enquiry, the Captain
of the great steamer Ripon, laid his telescope down, and
took hold of the ladies and gentlemen by the arm and
shoulders, and requested that they would not be so partial
to only one side of the boat, as it might dry one side of
her boiler, endangering his life, as well as theirs. "Now,"
said the Captain, "do you all see that tall, monumental
pillar, reaching upwards to the right of those barracks,"
when answered in the affirmative, he said, "That is Pompey's
Pillar, to the left is the Pacha's palace." This was indeed
the great city of Alexandria. Here it was Diogenes built
the great temple of Diana; and over it suspended her in
the air, by attractive and non-attractive metals, such as
loadstone and others. We are coming near, and the camel
boys and donkey drivers are more numerous than any other
class. Having gone a quarter of a mile through mud, I am
at the hotel, but I would as soon be any where else, for the

Pompey's pillar: The obelisk in Alexandria constructed as a monument
to Pompey, who was slain there.

accommodation is sickening.   A man and camel is standing at the door, with a bullock skin full of butter for the
landlord. . The landlord requested him to uncamel it, and
bring it in, after which he plated some of it for dinner.   I
enquired where this butter was made, and the Bedouin told
me it was made in the desert, and in recommending it, he
said it was good because he made it himself.   But the most
disgusting information I got of the origin of this butter,
was, that it was made from camel's milk, and this very
camel was one of the milch camels.   The landlord came to
know how we liked our dinner, and the Rev. Levi Tucker,
of Boston, Mass., enquired about this butter, and mine host
stuck his finger in the butter, and tasted thereof.   I was
eating a piece of roast beef at the time, but I could not
refrain from turning it over to ask myself, "might it not
be camel's meat," though I could get no answer.   After
dinner, four of us Americans, headed by the Rev. Levi
Tucker, called to see his most serene highness, the Pacha
of Egypt.   We stood before his palace in the court, about
an hour, after which the dragoman returned from the
interior of the palace and inquired of us if we were the
President, I told him not quite.   He then told us that his
serene highness had no complaint to make of us for
calling on him, and furthermore, that he had no objection
to our looking over the gardens, and at the walls of the
palace, and the stable doors.   Mr. Fellowes, of New Orleans,

lit a cigar, Mr. Elliot, of South Carolina, threw a quid of tobacco among the flowers, and I plucked a rose, and the Rev. Levi Tucker, so far descended from his gravity, to joke by saying, "you will all be fined, look sharp!"

This city was built by Alexander the Great, more than than three hundred years before Christ. It is on the Nile where it flows into the Mediterranean sea, but hardly any of its ancient splendor remains to point its site, save Pompey's Pillar, which is an immense stone column. Some parts of its walls are traced, and a few gates of granite marble are left to mark its spaciousness. Here used to pass the treasures of the Indies, but since the discovery of the route, via the Cape of Good Hope, only the mails traverse the Red sea, the Desert, and the Nile. Alexandria is the sea-port of Egypt, and Egypt is a province of Turkey. The Pacha pays the Sultan millions of treasure to rule this land himself, and also binds himself to furnish so many men in time of war, and is bound to lead them on the field if required. The present Pacha is said to be a foreign Prince, who fought his way to the throne. He lives here one part of the year, and the other at Cairo, the Capitol of Egypt. Cairo is about 275 miles from Alexandria, and as the English mail from the Indies comes there from towards the Red Sea to this place, they are now building railroads here, to facilitate conveying it to and from England and India.

EGYPTIAN KINGS OF OLDEN TIMES.

ALEXANDER the Great, after having extended his conquest to the Indies, returned to Babylon and there died in the thirty-third year of his age. Byron, who died at this age, pronounces it fatal to genius. We will not class our Savior with men of genius, as it would not be a just comparison to his superior talent or grace, but, if what Byron says about the turn of genius be true, there can be little argument against him when these specimens can be taken into consideration. After this great man's death at Babylon, his empire was divided among the next great men of the earth, and the Egyptian division fell to the Ptolemies. They were a great family of the upper part of the Nile, perhaps the Thebiad, and are known to us as Ptolemy 1st, 2d and 3d, &c. These kings were very learned, for they possessed the library of Alexandria, and which Caliph Omar burned containing 700,000 volumes of manuscript. For six months they burnt books instead of wood to heat the water they bathed in. The word Ptolemy means a class of kings. The emperors of Rome were known successively as Cæsars.

The Persians as Darius, just as the Louises of France were under the designation of one, two, and three.   These titles of the throne originated with the great and kingly family of Pharaohs.　Pharaoh Hophra is the famous Pharaoh that we are acquainted with in the scriptures.　Pharaoh Necko is another celebrated Pharaoh.　The present Cairo of Egypt, was then the Capitol of the greatest kings of the the earth, the Pharaohs.　It is still a magnificent city for its age.　Its population is variously estimated to be from 175 to 300,000.　Some as fine edifices are found here as in any part of the East.　It was the Memphis of old.　Here it was that Pharaoh dwelt when he marched in pursuit of Moses, when the cloud stood between them; here it is he is, to day, a mummy, if he was not embalmed in the Red Sea, but distinguished not; here it is the famine raged furiously and men sold themselves for food to Joseph; here it was that Moses had the power to turn ashes into dust, that flew over the land with the rapidity of a lightning flash, and infested the body of man with boils, and still the king loved the spot too well to give up one single foot of his powerful sway.　Here it was that Greece and Italy were schooled in all that they excelled; here it was that Moses obtained his fundamental rules of governing nations of people, for he was "learned in all the learning of the Egyptians," and where was more? and here it is some one thing is found that all the Savans' talent cannot conjecture the design of its structure, I mean the Pyramids. I was there to day, and gazed upward 470 odd feet in the air at its top. I say it because it is only necessary to see one to be confounded and awe struck. It is a spacious mass of solid layers of stone, one upon the other, and each from 25 to 32 feet in length.

What the great kings of Egypt had such a tremendous mass of stone so systematically put together for, is a mystery to all the learning of our time, and still we know it must have been for no ordinary freak of talent, intelligence and power, such a structure was reared. The old historians tell us it took twenty years to build one, with a force of 100,000 hands. These one hundred thousand men were relieved every three months by another hundred thousand. These stones were hewn from the mountains in the desert. It took ten years to make a causeway on which to bring these immense stones to the building. Each stone was originally adorned with engravings of animals, but now there is no vestige of them. The two largest in Egypt, and perhaps in the world, are these two here before Cairo. My dragoman insisted on my crawling in and seeing the wonders, but I could make nothing out of its hollow. It was lined with leather winged bats. If they were the sepulchre of kings, their bodies are long gone, though secure they might have been. In going to these Pyramids, one walks over a pavement of dead bodies. I sunk in the sand, one hundred yards from the pyramid of Cheops, and my foot caught in the ribs of a buried man, which I afterwards learned to be a mummy. Oh, mummy! when the side of the mountains was filled with the dead in old times, it was usual to take out the oldest corpse and put them beneath the earth, and in consequence, the whole plain, from the pyramids to Cairo, some six or seven miles, is macadamized with dead Egyptians, perhaps some kings and queens. I find that Pachas are reverenced here according to their wealth. If you ask an Egyptian whether said Pacha is a great man or not, he compares him to Pachas of a like means. The Pacha has all the learned men of the land around him. They now, as of old, carry their inkhorn tied to their waistband. No king, perhaps, of the earth is so absolute in will over his people as the present Pacha of the Turkisk empire. The kings of old time, no doubt, were more powerful in their absolute sway. When Thebes had one hundred gates undecayed, she could send to war, two millions of men. Such were Egyptian kings of olden time, though black.

Such were Egyptian kings of olden time, though black: Dorr's understated way of writing about black identity is again evident here. His intervention about blackness comes at the end of a long discussion commemorating the Egyptians.

TRAVELING ON THE NILE EIGHT HUNDRED MILES.

THE boat I obtained at Alexandria, was made like a keel boat. The cabin consisted of four bed rooms with a saloon in the centre. This cabin occupied the centre of the hull of the keel, but it left space outside all around, and more at each end than at the sides. The fourteen Arabs and one captain, called Reice, would either be pulling the boat all day, or managing the sail to advantage. When the breeze blew up the Nile, they would hoist the sail and take advantage of the wind. We paid them for the boat, men, and their own food, 250 pounds for the trip, but if the trip was not made in seventy days, and it is 800 miles, we then had to pay them so much for each day over, besides this, every few days the Reice would come into the cabin for bucksheesh; we were annoyed at every stopping place for bucksheesh. The Indian of North America would translate bucksheesh "gim E money."

Our cookery was at the bow of the boat, a small space of four feet square, and our cook was an Italian of Rome. We paid him two dollars a day, because he was a European, and could not work for less, and by the way, Arabs cannot cook, and will not, for any price, cook such food as we had. Our best meat was smoked pork, and they detest this meat. Nearly every man on our boat was named Achmit, or Mahommed; but the Reice's name was Marmound. The Reice was a good old man, I have often felt as if it would afford me great pleasure to sketch his profile, when, along about noonday, he would stop our boat without consulting us, to have his head shaved. The head shavers at all the little dirt villages, would keep a look out for boats, and be ready on the bank, to shave the captain's head, and make one cent.

The speculators of the Nile could always be found on the banks at the villages, waiting to sell a goat, a chicken, or an egg. When we would stop a minute or two at a village, every few seconds, women or men would come in great haste to sell, each one trying to beat the other, some dates, cloves, or chickens. Some places, when the boat was shoving out, some great, fat and lazy Arab would come blowing and panting to the edge of the Nile with one single egg, that he had been waiting for the hen to lay. One man, to make up a dozen, squeezed an old hen until her egg bag emitted a yelk, which I refused to take as an egg. One Arab brought us some young crocodiles he had dug out of their nest, even while the old one was chasing him. To believe what an Arab says when trying to sell anything, would be a sublime display of the most profound ignorance a man could be guily of. I have seen Arabs, however, professing an artful talent that I have no reason to believe can be found in the whole United States. I have reference to what is called snake charming.

Yesterday an Arab came aboard with a basket on his arm, and he was literally covered or clothed with live snakes. They were crawling over his shoulders, arms, breast, and whole body in general, and his head was an emblem of Discord. Serpents lôoked in all directions, while their forked tongues signaled their wrath, like little flashes of lightning. This was a "snake charmer," and we concluded we would test his skill, and gave him a quarter to go to the mountains and call out of the rocks some of his prey. Having arrived, he sang a melancholy strain like that of a dove in spring time, occasionally raising his voice like a lonely crane, and after ten or fifteen minutes of this proceeding, brought some three serpents from the crevices of the rock, and quietly walked to them and they crawled on his arm. He offered to guarantee one crawling on me without biting, but I was not willing to make any contract to that effect. He returned to the boat with us, and one of our Arabs, who was a very incredulous man, told us that the "rascal" was possessod of no power at all over the wild serpents, but had placed these serpents there before, and that they were taught to come when called. But this Arab of ours was jealous of the interesting enter- tainment we enjoyed. The charmer knew not where we were taking him until we told him to call the snakes. The Reice of our boat was afraid the charmer would get too much bucksheesh, and called on us in our cabin to inform us, that some months before he had seen this man with the same serpeuts, and I asked him how he distinguished the serpents, and he said, "by their color." He gave me to understand, that though we were very learned this rascal could fool us, but with him it was very different. He said that "old Marmond's beard was white, but few men knew more than he did," He appealed to our generosity, to keep some of the bucksheesh, "don't want the rascal to get all the bucksheesh."

At night the jackalls are quite noisy. Two came within fifty yards of our boat, and played their howling notes some time. No Arab takes notice of jackalls, foxes, or crocodiles. I went into six sugar houses on the Nile, and all owned by the Pacha. No man can show his money here without getteng it borrowed. The man who refuses to loan it to the Pacha when asked, cannot live. A wise man and bis money must part.

THEBES AND BACK TO CAIRO.

Two great streams rises in the Mountain of the Moon, in Abyssinia, and unites in Nubia, and flows through Egypt, and makes what we call "The Nile." This splendid old stream flows on gradually as in the days of Pharaoh, and Jupiter Hammon; splendid, because in those days its banks were walled with rich cities. The remains of Thebes stand like Catskill mountains, unshocked. I mean the remains, the renowned Memnonian, Luxor and Carnack. The tall columns of the Memnonian is here like untold riddles to be explained. The paintings are as bright to-day as any modern picture I have seen in the Louvre, at Paris. The carved chariots on the walls convey the idea, "I see Remesees and Pharaoh's on the battlefield." These chariots seem to have carried only two or three warriors with their spears in the battle. On the outside wall of this temple is carved, the exact likeness of a "man's individual part," varying from 6 to 13 inches in length, and hanging beneath each is two balls, seeming to be connected like the two big parts of a heart, and both gradually sloping down together. It is supposed, that cutting off these parts of man was the punishment or qualification required to degrade those gents of the Remesee court, who were too polite to the ladies. But why gallant gentlemen should be treated so I shall leave for the conjecture of the learned reader. Some light may be thrown on this subject by reference to the preceeding page, on Constantinople's manner of preparing gentlemen's nature for taking ladies to the baths.

These great temples are situated so that it takes a man many days to see them. They are on different sides of the Nile. Carnack is a tremendous mass of splendid ruins. Owls and foxes dwell within; and I saw a pretty bird, half asleep, that a man told me was a whip-poor-will. It is no pleasant thing to stop in these ruins a few hours alone, unless a man was possessed of no imagination at all. On one of the splendid painted broken columns that ran up through the hall or court of the unapproachable Pharaoh, Ptolemy, or Remese, a fox or hawk had been breakfasting on a rabbit, and martins had their nests perched on the side of the spreading columns that supported the beams of solid stone, of 12 feet wide and 20 long, over head. These ruins were sights of wonder to behold. Thebes could send to war 20,000 men from each of her hundred gates, making in all two millions of men. But to-day her walls cannot be found; we know her but by Carnack, and the rest of her temples, and the stadium of the Nile.

England and America has a consul here. He is a colored
man named Mustapha. He insisted on us taking dinner
with him before we left, and so we did. He had what is
called a fashionable Egyptian dinner of to-day. The goat
was cooked whole, and in a standing posture, and when
placed on the table, uncarved, the strongest fingered man
gets the best part with more ease and facility than the
weaker. Whoever has seen a skinned calf's head hanging
by a butcher's stall, can imagine how melancholy this
cooked goat's head looked.

Mr. Mustapha had no chairs or tables, but he had ample
room round the tray in the middle of the floor, where this
goat is placed. We all squatted as well as possible and
dined at nine o'clock at night; each one of us had hold of
Mustapha's goat at the same time. The Consul was indeed
skilled in obtaining long pieces of tenderloin. If he is as
well posted in diplomatic affairs as in finding tender parts
of a goat, he will do honor to England and America, or
Memphis of old. About 12 o'clock Mustapha said, "all
the dinner was eaten up, and now we would have some
dancing." The girls were called in, and they stocked their
bodies, and made a general preparation with their bells
tied to their waist. This was called tuning up. They
went off in their different strains, as you have heard three or
four sleigh turnouts, one after the other, and all getting together. Such a jingling; such screwing in and out of bodies;

such a gesturing ; and such a quivering of the bodies from
their necks to their knees, is only to be imagined.   One girl
stuck her head between her legs in front, whilst another
done the same over backwards.   A few minutes afterwards,
we eat some dates, smoked some pipes, and drank some
arrack, a liquid used here as we use whisky, brandy, and
gin, to raise the spirits.   The feast over, Mustapha informed
us that it was usual to pay his cook and waiter for their
services.   The next day he also informed us that it
was usual to pay him for being our consul, as he performed
this service for our government gratis.   This is his short
cut to the meeting house of distinction and gain.   We paid,
hoisted our sails, rowed away, and arrived in three weeks
afterwards, back to Cairo.

CAMELS, THROUGH THE DESERT.

FOR three of us, eighteen camels were procured, to convey us, provisions and tents, through the desert. To every camel was a master, who loads and unloads food and water.

The remainder of my travels will only be discribed as objects are found: no comments on their past or future.

Having at ten o'clock, the first time in my life, mounted a camel, I found it hard work to hold to the old riggings on his back. We went out on the commons to the east of Cairo, and turned the head of the camels towards Suez, on the Desert, and awaited their own movements. The youngest went out in all directions, as far as a quarter of a mile off; they would follow one another a few minutes, until they would lose confidence in the ability of the leader to perform his duty, and take the direction of another. After half an hour spent in this way, some of the young leaders would wait and look at the old camels and dromedaries until they would come along side, and wait quietly until the older would take the lead, and in five minutes the whole caravan from all directions would pull for his course, like the different branches of a flock of wild geese that had

been disturbed by some unnatural disturbance; in twenty
minutes all would be in a straight line for Palestine. At
five o'clock in the evening we camped for the night, and
while supping before our tent doors, the English mail caravan came along from Suez with the India mail, some 400
camels; they had left the red sea the day before, and were
getting along very well.   The English are great people to
meet in a strange place, as they take pleasure in imparting
all the news likely to add to ones comfort.   They asked us
about Her Majesty's government, and also about French
feelings.   We offered them something to drink, which they
refused, and bade us good day and went a couple of hundred
yards farther and camped.   Next morning they were off
before we waked up.   The next day we arrived at the red
sea, crossed over, and wended our way to Mount Sinai.
We found, at the base of Mount Sinai, two Bedouins, like
lost men from their tribe, looking about as if they were
hunting something in their lonesome vallies.   They rode
Arab steeds instead of camels, as we did in the Desert.   I
had always believed that the desert was an arid sandy
plain, but I found it more hill than plain.   Occasionally
we would see a couple of gazelles on the mountain crag, but
always ready to run.

   We stayed at the convent of St. Catherine some days
with the old monks, and bought some treasures of them in
the way of manna, put up here for pilgrims in a little tin

box, like mustard boxes, and also some canes of different
kinds of shrubs growing round about here. It takes about
an hour to wake the monks up from their studies, breakfast
or sleep. They lowered a sort of a hamper basket for us to
seat ourselves in, one at a time, and they pulled us up.
Next morning we prepared our luncheon for an ascent;
about twelve o'clock we reached the top where Moses held
the stones. The guide showed us many little altars and
curious places, said to be sacred places, to different ages of
which he named. I could plainly see that his information
was merely traditionary, without the least shadow of history
for support. As we ascended, he showed a hole in the
ground where the sons of Levi buried their dead. I asked
him how he knew this was the history of this hole, and he
said that a powerful Sheik told him this. He meant the
chief of a tribe of Bedouins. They are called Sheiks.
The Sheik who gave this important information was a very
powerful Sheik, and consequently, his opinion carried
great weight, though he could not read. He often settles
questions more important than this to the Arabs. The
next day, while branching out from Sinai and the Red Sea,
we encountered a desperate tribe of Bedouins, who demanded of us a bonus, in genuine coin, for permission to
travel through this territory. We refused to pay, and the
Sheik declared that we should. Our guide, whose name
was Como, said many years ago he traveled along the

range with one Dr. Robinson who wrote a book, and was attacked by this rascally Sheik before, and refused to pay then, and would refuse now. He bullied up to the Sheik, and told him he would report him to the authorities of Hebron, who would send his complaint to Constantinople, to the Sublime Porte. The Sheik was intimidated, and rode off in the Desert towards Petra. After thirty-five days in the Desert, we came to Hebron, the burial ground of Ahraham, Isaac, and Jacob. Here we quarantined for three days. After traveling all these thousands of miles, the Arabs would not let us enter the mosque built over these distinguished men's bodies. Our camel drivers could enter, they were Arabs, and would not defile the mosque.

JERUSALEM, JERICHO, AND DAMASCUS.

PASSING by the mosque whose treasure is the Patriarch's bodies covered with golden robes, the boys and women threw stones at us, that we might know we were approaching too near their sacred dead. They pride themselves on these sacred relics, and allow no man to pass by without seeing their fidelity displayed. Our drivers explained to us all they knew of the magnificence inside, but that was poor explanation and satisfaction, as it had also to be translated. As we left the city on our way to Jerusalem, we were shown some two or three olive trees nearly three thousand years old. About an hour after emerging from the city of Hebron, we met an Arab, and inquired the distance to the Holy City, and he said, "about half a day's camel ride." All miles are counted here by some animal's hour's travel. At one o'clock we were passing over rolling mounds adorned with olive trees. One was higher than the rest, and from its summit I saw Jerusalem only half a mile ahead. Its towers were few and scarce, and its walls were parched and charred. The mosque of Omar's dome glittered in the sun beam, and this Mahommedan sanctum towered above all the other buildings in this city, that was once the "glory of the world," because of its godliness. Yes, the mosque of the Turk looked down upon our glorious sepulchre, as it were with contempt. I made my way straight to our humble edifice, and fell upon the marble slabs that once entombed the flesh and blood of the greatest man ever tabernacled in a body of flesh. In the middle of the Latin Church, which means the church we christians of the world built over Calvary, is another small house like a large sepulchre, such as I have seen in New Orleans, or *Pere la Chaise*, at Paris, and in this little house are the sides, bottom, and cover, of the tomb of our Savior, just as it was taken from the earth and placed on this stone floor, before this little house and the large church were built around it. Two men were inside of the little house, one at each end of our Savior's tomb, giving wild flowers to the visitors. These flowers are fresh, and placed daily on the tomb beside the burning candles, that burn night and day on this consecrated marble tomb. An English lady, who came in before me, was prostrated on the floor, kissing the tomb with great devotion. She was a lady of rank who had pilgrimed here, and now had given way to her devoted feelings towards the dull, cold marble that once, in the midst of thousands of enemies, our Savior had lain in, uncorrupted, though bleeding and mangled.

Yes, the mosque of the Turk looked down . . . contempt: In this assessment, Dorr concurs with most Western travel writers who felt appalled at the proximity of the mosque and the sepulchre. Melville recorded his own concern in *Clarel*.

The monks were passing to and fro in all directions. The best place to locate for a short time, is in the convent attached to the church; they make no charges against a pilgrim, but no pilgrim can come here unless rich, and no rich man will go away without giving something to so sacred a place as the tomb of our Savior.

These monks are strict in all their rules, and allow none to be treated with indifference; they allow no chickens, ducks, cats, or dogs in the convent; as by their courting habits they might lead the mind of man from spiritual reflections, to groveling desires. These are undisputed facts, and I got them from the lips of a monk's aid. I walked round the walls of this celebrated city in one hour and a quarter, though when Titus took it, it contained about 2,000,000 souls. But as Jerusalem was considered by the Jews impregnable, the people from all the villages round about came here for safety. This accounts for its having so many people when taken. I am mounting a small Arab steed to go to Bethlehem. I can see it from here. In an hour after leaving Jeruselem, I passed by the tomb of Lazarus, and rode up to the walls of the convent at Bethel. It was closely shut on all sides. Our guide demanded in an authorative tone and air for entrance. A bare footed monk unlatched the door, and we walked in, and were carried direct to the altar built over the manger. We saw burning candles and flowers strewn around. We came out and wended our way towards Jericho, it could be seen in the distance. We came to a spring whose water was running freely, and the guide had the impudence to tell me that the cause of this water running so freely, was because the jawbone that Sampson fought so bravely with was buried here. He had told me another absurd story about Jeremiah's cave, but I was not inclined to believe anything I heard from the people about here, because I knew as much as they did about it. I came to Jerusalem with a submissive heart, but when I heard all the absurdities of these ignorant people, I was more inclined to ridicule right over these sacred dead bodies, and spots, than pay homage.

The same evening I camped at Jericho, about a hundred yards from where the Jordan empties into the Dead Sea. We took a bath in the Jordan, and tried some of its water with *eau de vie*, and found it in quality like Mississippi water. Then before we dressed, we took another in the Dead Sea. I cannot swim, but I could not sink in this sea; it is a strong brine of sulphur and salt, and stronger in holding up substances than the Mediterranean or the Atlantic. No living creature can live in it; the Jordan washes an immense quantity of small perch-like fish into it, but they instantly die, and are thrown out on the banks of the sea within twenty feet of the Jordan. The Jordan is frightfully rapid, but so narrow that a child could throw a stone across any part of it within a mile of the sea. Rabbits and birds are plentiful here; in the shrubbery in the valley of the Jordan I killed doves and quails enough for supper. Jericho is not worth mentioning, as there is not even a temple here left by time. The ground is covered with broken bricks and stones.

Having stayed in the city of Jerusalem seventeen days, I leave it, never wishing to return again, and am now leaving the wall, Calvary, Moriah, and Olivet, to see Gallilee, Tabor, Nazareth, and Damascus. I saw the sea, as no doubt it was when the whale vomited; I saw the little house where water was turned into wine, I saw Tabor, ascended and took my chances with the wild boar; I returned from Tabor to Nazareth, where I had left my baggage and provisions; eat some camel's meat. The soldiers were preparing for army stores, and I hurried on to Damascus to hear something about the decrees of St. Petersburg against the sublime Porte. The Turks all through Palestine were preparing for war; they said this year, 1853, was going to be a memorable one; the crescent and the cross were to shine gloomily, for the hungry Russian bear was seeking food beyond his lair. About the 1st of July I arrived at the Paradise-plain City of Damascus, and bought a blade. I bought some silks, and old swords, celebrated as Damascus blades were, with one I cut a half a dollar into two pieces. The ambassadors of different nations were inform-

---

The Turks all through Palestine were preparing for war: Turkey declared war on Russia in 1853, initiating the Crimean War, in which Russia suffered heavy losses.

ing their country's subjects that it was best to be among the missing, and said that some Russians were here yesterday, but were now gone to parts unknown. These ambassadors were more frightened than their subjects; one said to Col. Fellowes and myself, ''as soon as the Sultan declares war, no christian will be allowed to pass the barrier of his boundary, and as this is said to be a quarrel on religion, every christian head might fall '' that is found where waves the little Turkish flag of the crescent and the cross.'' I packed my trunk, paid my bill, and left Damascus and its sights, and traveled towards the Mediterranean. I looked at my old Damascus blade, and thought of those sharp scymaters, like reap hooks, and as I could see one in my imagination, I felt all over, and spurred towards Joppa.

CONCLUSION.

I am now letting loose the thread of my knowledge; the broach is turning from me to pull away the end, and with it the satisfaction that though its a hard broach to tie to, I have spun *no yarn.* The reader that only believes what he can see, through a limited source of facts, is always losing time and money, to read another man's knowledge; but the one who is always seeking to add to the stock of knowledge which he already has, is sure to gain time and knowledge in the stride of life.

On my way to Joppa I passed through Lebanon, took a glance at the old cedars, which I can pronounce nothing but spruce pine. I brought some of the burrows home to New Orleans, and they received from my friends the appellation above. An old man close to the little group of cedars, offered me his virgin daughter for the sum of twenty-five dollars; he seemed to be in great want of money. I hurried to Acre, and looked at its strong walls, and heard its foolish citizens talk of the impossibility of any nation being strong enough to take it.

I am now letting loose . . . spun *no yarn:* This is the only time Dorr evinces the concern for authentication that was so prevalent in African-American narratives. Yet Dorr's concern, unlike that in most African-American narratives, is not about proving his writing abilities to a skeptical readership but rather, like most Western travel writers, about the facticity of his accounts.

Jaffa is the present name of Joppa. It was formerly the sea port town of Palestine ; it has suffered much from being the gate city of Syria. Here, at Jaffa, I took passage to Marseilles, France, and arrived there just as the emperor of Morocco, who had been visiting France, was departing, himself and retinue, for Morocco, the Capitol of his Empire. I arrived back to Paris before the last of July. On the second day of September, the Franklin backed out from the wharf at Havre, France, with a splendid trip of passengers for New York city. Among these were Charles W. March, private secretary of Mr. Webster, and Geo. W. Kendall, the traveling editor of the New Orleans Picayune. They seemed to me the happiest men aboard ; they eat their good dinners, drank their good wines, and came on deck and inquired of me my opinion of thousands of little things that I thought hardly worth noticing. I am passing by England and Wales for home, my journey must be considered done. Youth is ever ready to be where it seems no advantage to him ; and it is a long time before he can surfeit on curiosity, enough to say, "alack, and well-a-day!" The aged are rough and ready implements of the world, they are too tightly riveted to their designs to let loose when they are absolutely in danger ; yes, Old Fogy goes on like a saw on a nail, determined to go through because he had the power, heedless of the consequences, and determined to make the nail suffer for attempting to impede his progress; he soon finds his sawing propensities broken, and much the worse for wear. But not so with youth. I feel in taking leave of this work, as if I was parting with an old and familiar friend that I could stay much longer with, but I am afraid to stay much longer lest I enhance its value as a friend. *A friend?* Yes, a friend!

James says that men of talent are often seen with many books before them, extracting their contents and substances. Were such men authors? No! but imitators; they wrote few impressions because few were made; they merely confirmed what others proved.

Like an anxious boy, in the ardor of anxiety to describe, I may fail, but I tell the thing as I saw it.

Should the reader think strange that I could find pleasure in these curious and strange places for a young man to be in, wherein they may occasionally find me, he must bear in mind that those are the only places and streams where flows the tide of curiosity from the mind of a youthful channel. There is no sameness about youth; like the clock when down, he must be wound up, or there can be shown no fine work in the machinery of a career of glory. Henry kindled his own fire, Washington paddled his own canoe, and for a bright manhood, youth must find his own crag on the mountain, rivet his eye of determined prosperity up the cliffy wiles of life, kick assunder impediments and obstacles, and climb on! When you hear *can't*, laugh at it; when they tell you *not in your time*, pity them; and when they tell you *surrounding circumstances alter cases*, in manliness scorn them as sleeping sluggards, unworthy of a social brotherhood.

All are obliged to unite when a question of *might* against *right* comes up, as it is now before the world. Dickens says, "no doubt that all the ingenuity of men gifted with genius for finding differences, has never been able to impugn the doctrine of the unity of man." He further says, "The European, Ethiopean, Mongolian, and American, are but different varieties of one species." He then quotes Buffon, "Man, white in Europe, black in Africa, yellow in Asia, and red in America, is nothing but the same man differently dyed by climate." Then away with your *can't*; when backed to the wall by the debator, you had better say *nothing* than *can't*. You had better say, as I say while taking leave of you, *au revoir*.

When they tell you *not in your time:* Dorr's language here echoes the radical David Walker.

SELECTED BIBLIOGRAPHY

NINETEENTH-CENTURY AFRICAN-AMERICAN TRAVEL NARRATIVES

Brown, William Wells. "The American Fugitive in Europe: Sketches of Places and People Abroad." In *The Travels of William Wells Brown*, ed. Paul Jefferson. New York: Markus Wiener, 1991.

Campbell, Robert. *A Pilgrimage to My Motherland: An Account of a Journey Among the Egbas and Yorubas of Central Africa in 1859–60.* New York: Thomas Hamilton, 1861.

Cary, Mary A. Shadd. *A Plea for Emigration; Or, Notes of Canada West.* Detroit: George W. Pattison, 1852.

Douglass, Frederick. *The Life and Times of Frederick Douglass.* New York: Bonanza Books, 1962.

———. *My Bondage and My Freedom.* New York: Arno, 1968.

Delaney, Martin. *Official Report of the Niger Valley Exploring Party.* New York: T. Hamilton, 1863.

Equiano, Olaudah. *The Interesting Narrative of the Life of Olaudah Equiano or Gustava Vassa, the African. Written by Himself.* London, 1789.

Griffin, Farah Jasmine, and Cheryl Fish, eds. *A Stranger in the Village: Two Centuries of African American Travel Writing.* Boston: Beacon Press, 1998.

Harris, Dennis. *A Summer on the Borders of the Caribbean Sea.* New York: Negro Universities Press, 1969.

Nesbit, William. *Four Months in Liberia; or, African Colonization Exposed.* New York: Arno, 1969.

Prince, Nancy. *A Black Woman's Odyssey through Russia and Jamaica: The Narrative of Nancy Prince.* New York: Markus Wiener, 1990.

———. *The West Indies: Being a Description of the Islands.* Boston: Dow and Jackson, 1841.

Smith, Amanda. *An Autobiography: The Story of the Lord's Dealings with the Colored Evangelist Containing an Account of Her Life Work of Faith, and Her Travels in America, England, Ireland, Scotland, India, and Africa, as an Independent Missionary.* New York: Oxford University Press, 1988.

Williams, Samuel. *Four Years in Liberia: A Sketch of the Life of the Rev. Samuel Williams; with Remarks on the Missions, Manners, and Customs of the Natives of Western Africa.* New York: Arno, 1969.

Critical Works

Adler, Judith. "Travel as Performed Art." *American Journal of Sociology* 94 (1989): 1366–91.

Andrews, William L. *To Tell A Free Story: The First Century of Afro-American Autobiography, 1760–1865.* Urbana: University of Illinois Press, 1988.

Baker, Houston. *The Journey Back: Issues in Black Literature and Criticism.* Chicago: University of Chicago Press, 1980.

Blassingame, John. *Black New Orleans, 1860–1880.* Chicago: University of Chicago Press, 1973.

Bourdieu, Pierre. *Distinction: A Social Critique of the Judgment of Taste.* Trans. Richard Nice. Cambridge: Harvard University Press, 1984.

Brown, Sharon Rogers. *American Travel Narratives as a Literary Genre from 1542 to 1832.* Lewiston: Edwin Mellen, 1993.

Brucolli, Matthew J. *The Profession of Authorship in America, 1800–1870: The Papers of William Charvat.* Columbus: Ohio State University Press, 1968.

Caesar, Terry. *Forgiving the Boundaries: Home as Abroad in American Travel Writing.* Athens: University of Georgia Press, 1995.

Clifford, James. "Traveling Cultures." In *Cultural Studies,* ed. Lawrence Grossberg, Cary Nelson, and Paula A. Treichler. New York: Routledge, 1992.

Elder, Arlene A. *The "Hindered Hand": Cultural Implications of Early African-American Fiction.* Westport, Conn.: Greenwood Press, 1978.

Fish, Cheryl. "Voices of Restless (Dis)Continuity." *Women's Studies* 26 (1997): 475–95.

Gates, Henry Louis. *The Signifying Monkey: A Theory of African-American Literary Criticism.* New York: Oxford University Press, 1988.

Mulvey, Christopher. *Transatlantic Manners: Social Patterns in Nineteenth-Century Anglo-American Travel Literature.* Cambridge: Cambridge University Press, 1990.

Peterson, Carla. "'Colored Tourists': Nancy Prince, Mary Ann Shadd Cary, Ethnographic Writing." In *"Doers of the Word": African-American Women Speakers and Writers in the North (1830–1880).* New York: Oxford University Press, 1995.

Porter, Dennis. *Haunted Journeys: Desire and Transgression in European Travel Writing.* Princeton: Princeton University Press, 1991.

Pratt, Mary Louise. *Imperial Eyes: Travel Writing and Transculturation.* New York: Routledge, 1992.

Said, Edward. *Orientalism.* New York, Pantheon, 1978.

Smith, Harold F. *American Travellers Abroad: A Bibliography of Accounts Published before 1900.* Carbondale: Library of Southern Illinois University, 1969.

Stowe, William W. *Going Abroad: European Travel in Nineteenth-Century American Culture.* Princeton: Princeton University Press, 1994.

Stuckey, Sterling. *Slave Culture: Nationalist Theory and the Foundations of Black America.* New York: Oxford University Press, 1988.

Williamson, Joel. *New People: Miscegenation and Mulattoes in the United States.* Baton Rouge: Louisiana State University Press, 1995.

TITLES OF RELATED INTEREST

Kamau Brathwaite
Roots

Charles W. Chesnutt
The Conjure Woman • *The Marrow of Tradition* • *The Wife of His Youth and Other Stories*

Harry J. Elam, Jr.
Taking It to the Streets: The Social Protest Theater of Luis Valdez and Amiri Baraka

Rudolph Fisher
The Conjure-Man Dies: A Mystery Tale of Dark Harlem • *The Walls of Jericho*

Édouard Glissant
Black Salt • *Poetics of Relation*

Lorna Goodison
Selected Poems

Robert Hayden
Collected Prose

Charles P. Henry, ed.
Ralph J. Bunche: Selected Speeches and Writings

Aida Hurtado
The Color of Privilege: Three Blasphemies on Race and Feminism

George Lamming
In the Castle of My Skin • *The Pleasures of Exile* • *The Emigrants* • *Season of Adventure* • *Natives of My Person*

J. Clay Smith, Jr., ed.
Rebels in Law: Voices in History of Black Women Lawyers

Stephen Caldwell Wright
On Gwendolyn Brooks: Reliant Contemplation